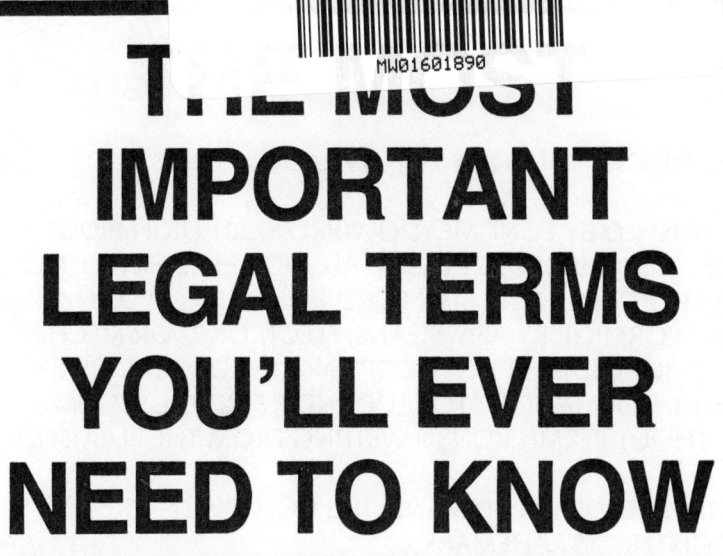

THE MOST IMPORTANT IMPORTANT LEGAL TERMS YOU'LL EVER NEED TO KNOW

Stanford M. Altschul, Esq.

LONGMEADOW PRESS

Stamford, Connecticut

COVER DESIGN BY KELVIN P. ODEN

INTERIOR DESIGN BY PAMELA C. PIA

LIBRARY OF CONGRESS
CATALOGING-IN-PUBLICATION DATA

ALTSCHUL, STANFORD M.
    THE MOST IMPORTANT LEGAL TERMS YOU'LL EVER
NEED TO KNOW / BY STANFORD M. ALTSCHUL. —
1ST ED.
    P.   CM.
ISBN 0-681-00583-1
    1. LAW—UNITED STATES—DICTIONARIES.   2. LAW—
UNITED STATES—POPULAR WORDS.   I. TITLE.
KF156.A48   1994
349.73'03—DC20
[347.3003]   94-26929
                                                  CIP

PRINTED IN THE UNITED STATES OF AMERICA
FIRST EDITION
0 9 8 7 6 5 4 3 2 1

PREFACE

I have represented clients in urban, suburban, and rural areas. In my conversations with clients, I have found that the general public does not always understand the language taught in law schools and used among attorneys. Often, clients use legal terms improperly, sometimes to their detriment, having picked up these words on television, radio or in newspapers without understanding their full meaning. It is also not unusual to hear these words used incorrectly in the media.

In my general practice, I have continuously tried to explain legal words and concepts to my clients in simple nonlegal language. In this book I have strived to communicate the meanings in this simple nonlegal language — so that the general public can become better informed and therefore better equipped in a litigious society.

Lawyers use special terminology to define precisely specific legal concepts. They are not using these words to confuse or frighten the public, but unfortunately this does occur. Many states have recently passed laws that require contracts to be written in plain English — a good trend.

However, even plain language agreements will contain words that the general public does not use. This is because our law relies on prior judicial interpretations of these words. By referring to these prior judicial decisions, attorneys and judges can learn the precise meaning of words that have evolved over the last three to four hundred years. The use of what appears to be another simpler word or group of words may result in a contrary interpretation — which would be detrimental to a client's interest.

I hope this book will open the eyes of the general public to legal language. To understand legal words and phrases is not to fear the unknown in a legal situation. I also hope that attorneys will read this book and realize not only that they must communicate to the public in clear language but that in instances where they must use precise legal words or phrases, they should not take their meanings for granted. Part of being an attorney is seeing to it that the clients understand the legal concepts that have brought them to the attorney.

Whenever a word or phrase appears in italics in a definition, the reader should be aware that the word or phrase is separately defined in this book.

Stanford M. Altschul
February 1, 1994

Acknowledgments

This book would not have become a reality without an editor, Pamela Liflander, who initially conceived the idea for it, then nurtured it along to completion. Her experience and suggestions were invaluable. I also want to thank my wife, Naomi, for her love and patience in bearing with me during the long hours of writing and reviewing the material. Finally, to my two office assistants, Barbara Whittier and John Carroll, who typed and retyped the manuscript, my thanks for their dedication to this enormous task.

A

ABANDONMENT — A ground for *divorce* in which one spouse leaves another without justification, without consent, and without the intent to return.

ABET — To encourage another to commit a criminal act.

AB INITIO — A Latin phrase for "from the beginning." Used to describe a marriage or *agreement* that was illegal at its start and thus is invalid.

AB TRUSTS — A transfer of assets to trusts by a married couple for the purpose of avoiding probate and minimizing or avoiding federal inheritance taxes.

ABORTION — The removal of a fetus prior to birth for the purpose of terminating a pregnancy.

ABSOLUTE AUCTION — An auction sale where the property is sold for the highest price bid. See *reserved auction*.

ABSTRACT — A report setting forth the name of the owner of *real property* and any *liens* against the *real property*, including but not limited to mortgages, unpaid taxes, recorded leases, *judgments* and easements.

ABUSE OF DISCRETION — The decision of a judge that is clearly unreasonable and arbitrary. The decision erroneously sets forth facts that are not in evidence or it sets forth misstatements of applicable law.

ABUSE OF PROCESS — A cause of action arising out of the improper use of a summons, subpoena, or other legal process.

ACCELERATION — A clause in a *note*, *bond*, *mortgage*, or loan *agreement* that causes the whole balance to become due immediately. This usually occurs when there is a default in the payment of an installment.

ACCEPTANCE — An agreement by a party to the terms and conditions of a contract that is proposed in the form of an offer by another.

ACCESSORY — A person who aids another person in a criminal activity.

7

ACCIDENT — The happening of an unexpected event.

ACCOMPLICE — A person who engages in a criminal activity with another.

ACCOUNTS PAYABLE — The debts owned by a business that are currently due.

ACCOUNTS RECEIVABLE — The outstanding payments due a business.

ACCORD AND SATISFACTION — An *agreement* between two parties to settle an outstanding dispute by a compromise.

ACCUSATION — A charge against a person concerning a criminal or illegal act.

ACCUSED — A person charged with a criminal activity.

ACKNOWLEDGMENT — A writing signed by a notary public. The notary declares the genuineness of the signature of a person.

ACQUIT — The verdict of a judge or jury that finds a person not guilty of a criminal offense.

ACTION — A claim of one party against another, set forth in a lawsuit.

ACT OF GOD — The occurrence of an event due to natural causes (such as a storm or earthquake), without the intervention of a human being.

AD DAMNUM — Latin for "to the damage." The paragraph of a complaint in a civil action that asks for monetary damages or other specific relief from a court.

ADDITIONAL INSURED — A party named in an insurance policy who is also covered by the policy, such as a landlord or lending institution.

ADMINISTRATOR — A man appointed by a court to gather and disburse the assets of a deceased person who died without a will.

ADMINISTRATRIX — A woman appointed by a court to gather and disburse the assets of a deceased person who died without a will.

ADMINISTRATOR WITH WILL ANNEXED — A person appointed by a court to administer an estate when there is a will but the executor named cannot or will not serve.

ADJOURN — When a judge sets another date for a legal proceeding.

ADJUDICATION — The *verdict* or *decision* of a *tribunal* that makes findings of fact and/or law in a legal proceeding.

ADJUSTER — A person employed by an insurance company who evaluates and attempts to settle *claims*.

ADMINISTRATION EXPENSES — The normal expenses incurred after a person dies, which include burial fees, payment of debts, payment of legal fees, and payment of commissions due administrators or executors.

ADMINISTRATIVE AGENCY — A governmental body established to regulate a particular activity; for example, the Federal Communications Commission regulates radio and television transmissions.

ADMINISTRATIVE HEARING — A trial in a court established by a governmental body to regulate a particular activity.

ADMINISTRATIVE LAW JUDGE — A judge appointed for the purpose of trying issues related to the function of a governmental agency.

ADMIRALTY — The laws governing the maritime industry.

ADMISSIBLE EVIDENCE — The evidence offered in an action that the jury and/or judge is permitted to hear and see.

ADMISSION — The act of not contesting particular facts that are set forth in a lawsuit.

ADOPTION — The court process by which a person or a couple take financial responsibility for and custody of a child. The child also becomes an heir to the person who is adopting the child. Generally, the consent of the natural parent(s) is required for an adoption.

ADOPTIVE CHILD — A child who has been offered for adoption and has been adopted by a person or couple.

ADOPTIVE PARENT — An adult who has agreed to adopt a child.

ADULTERY — An act of cohabitation between a married person and a single person.

ADVERSARY — A person who opposes another in a legal proceedings.

ADVERSARY PROCEEDING — A trial where two or more parties oppose each other and each have an opportunity to present their side of a dispute.

ADVERSE INTEREST WITNESS — A witness who is called to testify by a party whose success in the lawsuit would be against the interests of the witness.

ADVERSE POSSESSION — A claim to the ownership of *real property* based on the assumption that this property was already part of your aggregate lot. Generally, state law requires the open use of the premises for at least a ten-year period.

AFFIDAVIT — A sworn statement made in writing and signed before a notary public. An intentional falsehood may be punishable as *perjury*.

AFFIRMATION — A statement in writing, under the penalties of *perjury*, in which a person declares the truth.

AGENCY — The agreement between a *principal* and an *agent* where the agent acts on behalf of the principal. A principal may be disclosed or undisclosed.

AGENT — A person who has an *agreement* with a *principal* to act on behalf of a principal. The agent can have the authority to bind the principal.

AGREEMENT — An oral or written contract between two or more parties whereby there is a union for a common purpose.

ALIEN — A person who is not a citizen of the country.

ALIENATION OF AFFECTIONS — A claim by one person against another that describes the interference in a loving relationship by a third party.

ALIMONY — The financial payments that one spouse must make to another spouse (or former spouse) resulting from a *separation* or *divorce agreement* or *decree*.

ALLEGATION — A claim or statement made by one party against another.

ALSO KNOWN AS (a.k.a., a/k/a) — A phrase used after a person's name if that person is known by another name.

ALTERNATIVE DISPUTE RESOLUTION — A trial of a case before a private tribunal agreed to by the parties so as to save legal costs, avoid publicity, and avoid lengthy trial delays.

ALTERNATE JUROR — A juror who is present for the entire trial with the understanding that he or she will not be involved in the jury deliberation unless an impaneled juror becomes sick or is otherwise unable to serve.

AMERICAN ARBITRATION ASSOCIATION — A private organization that provides hearings for *litigants* who both agree to *alternate dispute resolution*.

AMICUS CURIAE — A person who has an interest in the outcome of a case who is not directly involved and wishes to submit a brief in the case. The court has discretion as to whether or not it will permit the brief to be submitted.

AMNESTY — A government order *waiving* a fine or penalty for a specific period of time.

AMORTIZATION — A sum that includes *principal* and *interest* and is used in the calculation of the repayment of loans and mortgages.

ANCILLARY ADMINISTRATION — If a person dies without a will, the *estate* is administered in the state of the permanent residence. If the person owned *real property* in another state, the *administrator* must file ancillary proceedings in that state in order to sell the real property.

ANCILLARY PROBATE — If a person dies with a will, the *estate* is *probated* in the state of the permanent residence. If the person owned *real property* in another state, the *executor* must file ancillary proceedings in that state so the executor can sell the real property.

ANNULMENT — A decree that terminates a marital relationship on the basis that the parties were never legally married; for example, if one of the parties was under age at the time of the marriage.

ANNUITY — An insurance policy that pays a sum of money over a specific period of time.

ANTITRUST — Laws that prevent businesses from fixing prices and thereby restraining competition.

ANSWER — The written response of a party in a lawsuit to the claim of the party that instituted the proceedings.

APPEARANCE — The act by which a party to a lawsuit submits to the *jurisdiction* of a *tribunal*. The party thus acknowledges that the court has the authority to render a decision in the action.

APPELLANT — The party that requests a higher court to overturn the decision of a lower court.

APPELLATE COURT — A court that has jurisdiction to review and thus affirm or reverse the determinations of a lower court.

APPURTENANT — An item of personal property that has been physically attached to real property.

ARBITRATION — An *alternative dispute resolution* system that is agreed to by all parties to a dispute. This system provides for private resolution of disputes in a speedy fashion.

ARBITRATOR — A person who has been authorized by the parties to a dispute to determine issues that are in conflict and render a binding decision. State laws provide that decisions of arbitrators can be entered as *judgements*. Appeals from decisions of arbitrators are severely limited.

ARMED ROBBERY — The taking of property of another with the use of a weapon.

ARRAIGNMENT — The proceedings in a criminal case where the accused is formally advised of the pending charges and given the right to plead either guilty or not guilty.

ARREARS — The sum of money past due on a debt, including the principal and interest.

ARREST — The restraining of the free movement of a person by another person. Arrest may be made by persons employed by a government such as police officers. Arrest can also be made by private citizens.

ARSON — The act of intentionally starting a fire with the intent of destroying life and/or property.

AS IS — A term used to indicate that whatever is being sold and/ or transferred is conveyed without any *representations* or *warranties*.

ASSAULT — The act of intentionally placing one in fear of being physically injured.

ASSESSMENT — A required sum of money to be paid by an identifiable group of people based on an agreement or a statute. The identifiable group of people includes, for example, the owners of a cooperative or condominium.

ASSIGN — The act of giving one's rights to money or property to another.

ASSIGNMENT — The agreement to give one's rights to money or property to another.

ASSOCIATION — A group of people who have come together voluntarily for a common purpose.

ASSUMPTION OF MORTGAGE — An agreement to pay an existing *mortgage* that was originally incurred by another. This usually happens when one purchases *real property* and agrees to continue to pay the monthly payments on an existing mortgage.

ASSUMPTION OF RISK — The act of committing an act knowing the dangers inherent in the performance of the act; for example, attending a baseball game results in assuming the risk of being hit by a foul ball.

ATTACHMENT — A method by which one person (a *creditor*) is able to restrain another from conveying or transferring money or property. The attachment results from either filing papers with the *county clerk* or serving papers on a person, an employer, or bank that has lawful possession of money or property of a *debtor*. The employer or bank would then be required to transfer the money to the creditor.

ATTEST — The act of swearing to the truth of a statement.

ATTORNEY — A person authorized by the courts of a state to give legal advice and represent clients for a fee.

ATTORNEY-CLIENT PRIVILEGE — Rule of law that says an attorney cannot disclose to anyone, including a court, information that is received from the client without the prior approval of the client.

ATTRACTIVE NUISANCE — The owner of *real property* is responsible for injuries sustained by *minors* when they enter the property in order to play with an object that draws them there. Object must be generally known to lure a minor. For example, an abandoned vehicle which is left on vacant land.

AUCTION — The sale of property to the highest bidder at a public forum.

AUTOMOBILE LIABILITY INSURANCE — An insurance policy that pays benefits to third parties who are injured accidently by the insured in the operation of his or her motor vehicle. It covers *personal injuries* and/or *property damage*.

B

BAD FAITH — The doing of an act with knowledge that a legal wrong is being committed.

BAIL — A sum of money set by a court in a criminal case, so as to ensure that the person accused of the crime will not flee the *jurisdiction* until the conclusion of the criminal trial. The money is paid to the court in cash or by filing a *bail bond* issued by an insurance company.

BAIL BOND — An insurance policy issued by an insurance company guaranteeing that a criminal will not flee the *jurisdiction* until the conclusion of the criminal trial. The insurance company will not issue a *bail bond* until it is fully collateralized by money or property.

BAILIFF — A court officer who assists the judge in the orderly functioning of a court.

BALLOON NOTE — A *note* that provides for monthly interest payments and has large payments of principal at specific times during the life of the note and/or at termination.

BANK CHECK — A check issued by a bank that is not drawn on an individual's account but on the actual account of the bank issuing the check.

BANKRUPTCY — A procedure under federal law that permits a person who is unable to pay *debtors* either to reduce the sum due to the debtors or to discharge the debts without payments. The bankruptcy court has the authority to review the *assets* and *debts* of the person declaring bankruptcy and to determine his or her ability to repay debts. The court generally arranges for the sale of all assets and distributes the funds to the *creditors*.

BAR ASSOCIATION — An organization of attorneys that promotes the interest of attorneys and seeks to promote goodwill between attorneys and the public.

BARGAIN & SALE DEED — A document that transfers all the rights of the seller of *real property* to the purchaser without any *warranties*. The purchaser has an opportunity prior to paying for the real property to search the title records and determine the seller's rights. The seller thus has no further responsibilities or obligations, once the sale takes place.

BASTARD — A person who is born out of wedlock; an illegitimate child.

BATTERY — The physical striking of one person by another without right or justification.

BENCH WARRANT — An order issued by a judge for the arrest of a person who has failed to appear at a specific time before the court.

BENEFICIARY — A person who will receive benefits from an *estate, agreement,* or *trust.*

BEQUEATH — A direction by the maker of a *will* giving specific property to a person.

BILL OF LADING — A document used by parties shipping goods to others by freight carriers. The document sets forth the terms that must be complied with before the actual delivery of the goods by the freight carrier.

BILL OF PARTICULARS — A written statement in a lawsuit detailing specific questions concerning the claim of a party.

BILL OF SALE — A written document that transfers *personal property* from one person to another.

BIRTH CERTIFICATE — A government record of a birth that states the name of the child and the parents.

BINDER — A short agreement between parties that binds the parties and provides that at a later time they will enter into a more formal agreement.

BODILY INJURY — The personal and physical injuries sustained by a party.

BOILERPLATE — The preprinted part of an agreement that is generally found in similar agreements.

BONA FIDE PURCHASER — A person who obtains a *note* by way of purchase who is not aware directly or indirectly that the *debtor* has a reason for not paying the note. For example, the *note* may have been given in purchase of a vehicle and the vehicle has since been found to be defective.

BOND — An agreement signed by a borrower that states the terms of a loan agreement, including the interest and the manner of repayment.

BOYCOTT — An act by one or more asking the public not to transact any business with another. It is a common activity associated with labor unions in their attempt to improve working conditions and the pay of their union members.

BREACH OF CONTRACT — An act that results in the unlawful termination of a contract. The party who breaches a contract will generally be responsible for paying all damages incurred by the other party.

BRIBERY — The act of giving money or property to an employee without the knowledge of that person's employer for the purpose of obtaining special treatment.

BRIEF — A written statement analyzing the facts of a case and the law that applies, prepared with the purpose of advising either a trial or appellate court of the position of one of the parties.

BROKER — A person who acts on behalf of another for the purpose of buying and selling property for which he or she receives a commission.

BULK SALE — The sale of all the assets of a business.

BURDEN OF PROOF — The responsibility of the prosecutor in a criminal case to convince a judge or jury that the defendant is guilty. It is also the responsibility of the claimant in a civil case to convince a judge or jury that the defendant owes the claimant money damages.

BURGLARY — The act of taking the *personal property* of another by forceful entry without right or justification.

BUSINESS RECORDS — The records of a business that are admissible in evidence at a trial because they were prepared by the employees of the business for the purpose of conducting the business.

C

CALENDAR — A listing of the cases awaiting trial before a court.

CAPITAL — The money used to purchase personal goods and services.

CAPITAL GAINS — The amount of profit resulting from the resale of *real* or *personal property*. The profit is determined by subtracting the seller's purchase price from the seller's sale price. All expenses of the sale are also deducted.

CAPITAL LOSS — The amount of loss resulting from the resale of *real* or *personal property*. The loss is determined by subtracting the seller's sale price from the seller's purchase price. All expenses of the sale are also added.

CAPITAL PUNISHMENT — The death penalty.

CAR LEASE AGREEMENT — The granting of the right to use an automobile for a period of months or years.

CAR RENTAL AGREEMENT — The granting of the right to use an automobile for a period of days or weeks.

CARRIER — A commercial freight shipper that delivers goods by land, sea, or air; term can also refer to an insurance company.

CASE — An action brought by one party against another to settle a dispute.

CASEBOOK LAW — The study of law in American law schools which is based on the reviewing of prior decisions of judges dealing with similar case facts.

CASE LAW — The law that has evolved by reading the decisions of judges. The higher the court the more weight is given to the judge's decision. The decisions are examined and analyzed for the purpose of determining how different judges view similar fact patterns.

CASUALTY LOSS — A loss that results in damage to property as a result of an accident and is usually covered by an insurance policy.

CAUSE OF ACTION — A claim by one party against another party resulting from an actual dispute between the parties.

CAVEAT EMPTOR — A Latin phrase for "let the buyer beware." This is a warning to purchasers that they must be cautious before paying money to a seller, because once they give the money to the seller they may have no means of getting it back if the goods are defective.

CENSURE — A statement by a governmental body that advises the public that a person under their jurisdiction, such as an attorney, physician, or accountant, has committed a wrongful act that has been officially noted. If the act is minor, there will be no penalty.

CERTIFICATE OF INCORPORATION — The document signed by a person establishing a corporation, which establishes the name of the corporation and its purposes.

CERTIFICATE OF OCCUPANCY — A document issued by a government agency attesting to the fact that a building has been constructed according to local building codes.

CERTIFICATE OF TITLE - A certification that a person is the official owner of a parcel of *real property*.

CERTIFIED CHECK — A check issued by an individual that is endorsed by the bank upon which the check is drawn. The bank automatically removes the funds from the individual's account and advises the payer of the check that it will be paid from this special fund when the check is deposited.

CERTIFICATE OF COMPLIANCE — A document issued by a government agency attesting to the fact that any changes or additions to a building after its initial construction have been made according to local building codes.

CERTIFICATION — A written statement saying that a photocopy of an attached order or document is authentic and is a true copy.

CERTIORARI — An application to appear before an appellate court to resolve a dispute between two parties.

CHAIN OF TITLE — The names of all persons who have owned a parcel of real estate since the establishment of written records.

CHALLENGE — A claim that a juror should not be permitted to serve on a jury because of some specific bias that will effect the juror's opinion.

CHARACTER WITNESS — A person who testifies as to the character of a party and his or her standing in the community.

CHARGE — The statement of the judge of the jury after the jury has heard all the evidence and is about to deliberate. The judge reviews all testimony and advises the jury as to the law they must apply in the case.

CHARITY — The giving to another of property or money without expecting anything of value in return.

CHATTEL — Any personal possessions that can be moved from place to place that are either mobile or stationary. *Real property* and buildings are not considered chattel.

CHATTEL MORTGAGE — A loan *agreement* that results in a *lien* against specific personal possessions, whether mobile or stationary.

CHECK — A promise in writing to pay another a specific amount of money. When the check is presented at the ban of the original party issuing the check, the amount is paid.

CHILD SUPPORT — A sum of money that a parent of a child must pay after a *divorce*. The failure to pay this amount may be punishable by placing the parent in jail, if they have the financial ability to pay.

CIRCUMSTANTIAL EVIDENCE — Facts that indicate that an act was performed. For example, finding the murder weapon in the possession of a person who has a motive to commit the crime.

CITATION — A court document that directs a person to appear before a specific court, at a specific time, for a specific reason.

CIVIL ACTION — A claim instituted by one against another arising out of a dispute that is not criminal in nature. The action usually requests either money damages or specific remedies.

CIVIL LAW — The law that governs the responsibilities and liabilities of parties in non-criminal cases.

CIVIL LIABILITY — A person's responsibility either to pay to another damages or to adhere to the directives of the court.

CIVIL PENALTY — A victim of a crime has the right to bring a civil action for monetary damages against the person who committed the crime.

CIVIL PROCEDURE — The statutory law that determines the rules that govern civil lawsuits. This includes all procedures from the institution of lawsuit to trial.

CIVIL RIGHTS — The antidiscrimination laws that protect all persons in the United States.

CLAIM — A *grievance* set forth by one party against another that has resulted in a dispute.

CLAIM OVER — The amount of *damages* the party being sued alleges they are owed by the *plaintiff*.

CLAIMANT — A person who brings a claim against another.

CLASS ACTION — One person representing a group that brings an *action* against a common party. Class actions are governed by statutory law. In many cases the members of the class are unknown and are requested to step forward and advise the parties of individual claims. For example, in lawsuits arising out of the use of a manufactured product which has harmed persons who have used the product.

CLEAN HANDS — A person who comes into court as a *litigant* who has done nothing wrong. A person who has been honest and has not sought any unjustified advantage.

CLEAR TITLE — A *title search* of *real property* that demonstrates a particular person has good *title* and that there are no *liens* against the property.

CLEMENCY — An act of the President of the United States or a governor of any state that reduces the sentence of a person who has been found guilty of a crime.

CLOSING — The date on which the *title* to either *real* or *personal property* is transferred from one person to another according to the terms of a previously signed contract of sale.

CLOSING ARGUMENT — The final speech in a trial in which each attorney sums up the case to the jury and/or judge so that a decision can be rendered in favor of the client. In criminal cases the prosecuting and defending attorney each try to persuade the jury of the guilt or innocence of the defendant.

CLOSING STATEMENT — A document issued after a sale of *real* or *personal property* that sets forth in detail the exchange of money for the property sold.

CLOUD ON TITLE — A finding in an examination of ownership that the owner does not have clear *title*. This usually results in the cancellation of the agreement to sell.

CODICIL — A change or addition of a *will*. Instead of redrafting a will, a specific paragraph is changed. Any change to a will must be executed before witnesses with the same formality as the execution of a will.

COLLATERAL ESTOPPEL — An act taken by an individual that prevents that person from alleging a claim or defense because of a contrary position.

COLLECTIVE BARGAINING — The negotiations between a *union* and an *employer* on behalf of the *employees*.

COLLISION COVERAGE — The automobile insurance policy that pays automobile property damage in the event of an accident.

COLOR OF LAW — The duties the government assigns law enforcement officers to perform.

COLOR OF TITLE — The exercise of the ownership of *real* or *personal property* by demonstrating that one person is the rightful owner.

COLLUSION — The act of two or more people acting together for a common purpose.

COMMERCIAL LAW — The law governing *checks, notes, bonds, chattel mortgages*, and general business transactions.

COMMERCIAL PAPER — A written note that contains all the provisions of a loan agreement.

COMMISSIONS — The monies due a broker when he or she has found a buyer for a seller and they have agreed on the price and the terms of sale.

COMMITMENT — An agreement by a lending institution to make a loan to a person subject to specific terms. It also sets forth the interest rate and the terms of repayments.

COMMITTEE — A person appointed by a court to look after the financial affairs of a *minor* or *incompetent*.

COMMON CARRIER — A company that provides regularly scheduled transportation of people or goods by land, sea, or air to all members of the public for the same rates.

COMMON DISASTER — An accident involving multiple deaths among members of the same family. A will may have a common disaster clause specifying inheritance in the event it can not be determined who was the last to die.

COMMON LAW — In all states except Louisiana, the common law is the basis of American law. This common law was implanted in our judicial system during the colonial period by the British. This system of law places great emphasis on the prior decisions of judges and the requirement that subsequent decisions follow the established precedents.

COMMON LAW MARRIAGE — The act of two people living together who identify the other as his or her spouse. Many states do not permit common law marriage by specific stature. These states generally recognize common law marriage that began in jurisdictions that permit common law marriages.

COMMUNITY PROPERTY — A term used in the states of Arizona, California, Nevada, and Texas that denotes property acquired by either spouse during the marriage that automatically becomes owned mutually, 50 percent by each spouse.

COMMUTATION — An act of the President of the United States or a governor of any state directing the reduction in the sentence of a person who has been found guilty of a crime.

COMPANY — A business entity owned by one or more parties.

COMPARATIVE NEGLIGENCE — A law governing accident cases that provides that the acts of negligence of both the *claimant* and *defendant* are to be weighed by the judge or jury. The percentage of negligence of the claimant reduces the monetary damages. The judge or jury determines the percentage of negligence of the claimant and the defendant.

COMPENSATION — The money or property received by a person for performing a requested act.

COMPENSATORY DAMAGES — The amount of damages due a *claimant* following an accident or breach of contract.

COMPETITION - The free marketplace in which businesses are permitted to sell goods at any price that they determine.

COMPLAINANT — The person who files a criminal charge against another. Once the criminal charge is filed, the district attorney prosecutes the case and the complainant is then addressed as a *witness*.

COMPLAINT — A document prepared for a civil lawsuit that sets forth the basis of the claim and the relief requested. In a criminal case, it sets forth the specific criminal statute charged and the basic facts that demonstrate the performance of the crime.

COMPLETION BOND — A document issued by an insurance company that guarantees to the owner of *real property* and/or a lending institution that a contractor will complete a construction job described in a written contract.

CONCUR — The practice in an appellate case that one judge writes a decision and other judges review the decision and agree with it.

CONDEMN — The right of a government to declare a building dangerous for use and to require the owner to remove or repair it.

CONDOMINIUM — A form of ownership of separate units in a multiple dwelling where each unit pays its own mortgage and taxes and has its own deed.

CONDONATION — The *waiver* of a grounds for divorce by a spouse. For example, if one spouse commits adultery and the other spouse, knowing of the adultery, consents to continue to have sexual relations with that spouse, this is considered a waiver of the particular incident that would have been grounds for divorce.

CONFESSION — A statement given by a person charged with a crime admitting to some or all of the elements of the crime.

CONFESSION OF JUDGMENT — An agreement between a debtor and creditor wherein the debtor agrees to the entry of a judgment against the debtor. The judgment can be entered immediately or at a future time if the debtor fails to make a payment.

CONFLICT OF INTEREST — The existence of opposing interests between the two parties. For example, a conflict of interest exists between a broker and the seller of *real property*. The broker wants to earn a commission by selling the property and the seller wants to receive the highest sum possible.

CONFLICT OF LAWS — If a case involves parties from two or more states, there may exist a dispute as to which state's law is applicable to the case, as laws may be different from one jurisdiction to another.

CONGLOMERATE — A parent corporation that owns a controlling interest in several other corporations selling divergent goods.

CONSENT DECREE — A *decree* or *order* of a court that is agreed to by all parties.

CONSENT JUDGMENT — A judgment entered in court that is agreed to by all parties.

CONSERVATOR — A person appointed by the court to supervise the assets of someone who lacks the mental or physical capacity to take care of his/her property.

CONSIDERATION — The right or benefit that one receives when entering into an agreement with another.

CONSIGNMENT — The delivery of goods to the seller for the purpose of resale. If they cannot be resold they must be returned. If they are sold the seller keeps a portion of the sale price as previously agreed and pays the balance to the party that gave him the goods.

CONSPIRACY — The act of one or more persons performing or planning an activity that is illegal.

CONSTRUCTION — A proceeding to have a court determine ambiguities in a contract or will.

CONSTRUCTIVE TRUST — A trust that is implied by the actions of the parties. For example, ownership in *real property* is transferred from one relative to another relative for the purpose of concealing who is the true owner. A trust is thus implied by the actions of the parties.

CONSUMER — The person who purchases goods at retail.

CONSTITUTION — The basic law of government that determines the powers of the executive, legislative, and judicial branches. The federal government and each state have their own constitutions.

CONTEMPT OF COURT — A ruling by a judge that a particular action of a party violated a previous order of the court.

CONTIGUOUS — Two parcels of *real property* that are in fact next to each other.

CONTINGENT BENEFICIARY — A person who is entitled to receive property in the event the original beneficiary is deceased, pursuant to a will or trust.

CONTINGENT FEE — A fee charged by an attorney that is a percentage of the amount recovered for the client. This type of fee arrangement is common in negligence claims.

CONTINUANCE — The act of a judge setting another date for a legal proceeding.

CONTRACT — An agreement between two or more parties to fulfill an obligation for money or property. The agreement is binding if it is mutually agreed upon and it is a lawful activity.

CONTRACT OF ADHESION — An agreement between two parties where one party has a substantial advantage, and thus the contract on its face is clearly unfair. For example, if a farmer agrees to sell his crop to only one party and the purchaser is not required to make the purchase, this contract then binds the farmer not to sell the crop to any other party.

CONTRACTOR — An independent party who performs a service in exchange for a payment of money. A contractor is not an employee (who receives wages) because he or she is not continuously supervised during the performance of the service.

CONTRIBUTION — The giving of money or property to a charitable institution where the donor receives no direct financial benefit other than the possible charitable deduction for tax purposes.

CONTRIBUTORY NEGLIGENCE — A law that states that a claimant in an action grounded in negligence cannot recover money if he contributed in any way to the happening of the occurrence and the resulting injury.

CONVERSION — The taking of the property of another without authority and without justification.

CONVEYANCE — The transfer of ownership of real or personal property from one to another.

CONVICTION — A finding by a jury or judge that a criminal is guilty of violating a specific criminal statute.

COOPERATIVE — A form of ownership of a unit in a multiple dwelling where each unit contributes money to pay its share of the common costs; that is, the mortgage and the taxes, based on the relative size of each unit.

COPARTNERS — Two or more persons engaged in a legal business activity with the aim of dividing the profits pursuant to a percentage determined in advance by agreement.

COPYRIGHT — A right given by statute that protects a writer or artist from the unauthorized duplication of his or her writing or artistic creation for a specific period of time.

CORONER — A person employed by a county government who investigates deaths that appear to be caused by other than natural causes.

CORPORAL PUNISHMENT — Physical punishment such as imprisonment, or beating a person.

CORPORATION — An entity created by statute that permits persons to own shares of stock. A corporation is treated under the law as a person; the individual shareholders are not responsible for the debts of the corporation unless they have personally guaranteed the debt.

CO-SIGNER — One who signs a loan agreement of another forming an obligation to pay the loan if the borrower does not repay it. A co-signer is jointly and separately *liable* for the debt.

COSTS — A sum of money for charges incurred in a lawsuit that are added to a court award. Generally, attorney fees are not considered costs except in rare cases where a statute permits them to be added.

CO-TENANCY — The ownership of property by more than one person.

COUNSEL — A person who is authorized by the courts to give legal advice and represents clients for a fee.

COUNTERCLAIM — Once a lawsuit is instituted, the party being sued can enter a claim against the party who brought the original suit.

COUNTY CLERK — A local government official who is charged with maintaining records of *real property* ownership, *liens*, *mortgages*, and court files. The county clerk also keeps records of all local corporations and partnerships.

COURT OF RECORD — A *tribunal* that employs a person to transcribe testimony during all hearings.

COURSE OF BUSINESS — A business activity that is ordinarily and customarily engaged in by a particular business. For example, the course of business for a bank is that it maintains back accounts and does not sell used cars.

COVENANT — An agreement among two or more parties that restricts one or more of the parties from engaging in an otherwise legal activity. A covenant can also affect future purchasers and the purposes for which real property can be used. This occurs when the covenant is recorded with the registrar of deeds and thus becomes a public record available to purchasers to read prior to purchasing the realty.

CREDIT — The loaning of money by one party to another with the borrower promising to repay the money with interest.

CREDIT CHECK — A method by which a lender of money determines the ability of a borrower to repay the loan. The credit check reviews all outstanding loans of the borrower and his or her record or repayment.

CREDITOR — One who lends money to a borrower with the expectation of the money being repaid with interest.

CRIME — An act that is prohibited by a specific statute. The statute must be in existence before the commission of the act.

CRIMINAL NEGLIGENCE — An accidental happening caused by one that demonstrates total disregard for life or property of another.

CROSS-CLAIM — If a lawsuit is instituted against more than one party, any of these same parties can assert a claim against the other party or parties who have been sued.

CROSS EXAMINATION — The procedure by which one party during a trial is given the opportunity to ask questions of the adverse party and its witnesses.

CUSTODY — A determination by agreement of the parents or by court order setting forth the residence of a minor. Any agreement between the parents can be changed by court order if the best interests of the child are not served by it.

D

DAMAGES — A sum of money awarded to a party by a court as compensation due from another party.

DEATH PENALTY — When the state exercises the right to take the life of a person convicted of violating a specific criminal statute.

DEAD MAN'S STATUTE — A rule of evidence that prohibits a person from testifying as to what a deceased person said if the testimony would result in a benefit to the person testifying. For example, a person can not testify that a decedent orally gave him property belonging to the decedent.

DEATH CERTIFICATE — A government record of a death that sets forth the name, address, and cause of death and is signed by a physician.

DEBT — An obligation to pay a sum of money to another resulting from a loan, the purchase of property, or the rendering of a service.

DEBTOR — One who owes money to another pursuant to an oral or written agreement.

DEBTOR IN POSSESSION — Applies to a party who has been unable to repay a debt and has been given the authority by a *bankruptcy court* to continue his or her business under court supervision. The court determines if the debtor's business can become profitable; if this is possible, the court establishes, with the creditors, a method of repayment of part or all of the debts.

DEBTOR'S PRISON — The confining to prison of persons who have not paid valid debts. This is not permitted in the United States except in the instance when a spouse fails to pay *alimony* and/or *child support.*

DECEASED — A person who has died.

DECEDENT — A person who has died.

DECLARATORY ACTION — An action instituted in a court that seeks to obtain an interpretation of an *agreement* or *statute* in order to resolve a dispute between parties.

DECREE — An order of a court.

DEDUCTION — The income tax laws provide that certain sums of money can be subtracted from your gross income to reduce the ultimate income tax. For example, payments to recognized charities can reduce gross income and are considered valid deductions.

DEED — A document used to transfer *real property*. Generally, deeds are recorded with a registrar of deeds, who may be the *country clerk*.

DEED OF TRUST — A document used to record a *lien* or *mortgage* against *real property* in Arizona, California, Nevada, and Texas.

DEFAMATION — Causing a person to be scorned or ridiculed by the community in which they reside. See *libel* and *slander*.

DEFAULT — The failure of a party to respond to a claim set forth in the lawsuit after being served with a summons, or the failure to appear for a trial set for a specific date.

DEFENDANT — The party in a lawsuit against whom an *action* has been instituted. There may be more than one defendant in an action.

DEFENDANT'S EXHIBIT — A document, photograph, or item of physical evidence offered by the defendant at a hearing. The court *reporter* numbers or letters each exhibit.

DEFENSE — The evidence and proof offered by a person against whom a *claim* or *charge* has been set forth.

DELIBERATION — The period of time that a jury or judge spends determining the facts in a particular case after they have heard all the testimony.

DEMAND NOTE — An agreement in writing to pay a sum of money to a lender, which is payable at any time the lender demands repayment.

DEMONSTRATIVE EVIDENCE — Evidence used at a trial that is physical in nature, such as a photograph, diagram, map, model, or some item of property.

DENTAL MALPRACTICE — A course of action demanding *damages* against a dentist that maintains the dentist has treated a patient in an improper manner.

DE NOVO TRIAL — The scheduling of a second, new trial in which the results of the original trial have no bearing.

DEPONENT — A person who either signs a written statement or gives an oral statement after first affirming or swearing to the truth of the same. An intentionally false statement in *perjury*.

DEPOSE — The act of recording the testimony of a party or witness prior to a trial. The testimony is used at the trial in the event the person is not available or is used to cross-examine the witness.

DEPOSITION — A proceeding prior to trial where a person testifies and the testimony is recorded for use during the trial. The deponent is sworn to tell the truth and an intentional false statement is *perjury.*

DESCENT — The laws determining the distribution of the assets of a deceased person in the event the deceased had no will.

DEVISE — A part of a will that sets forth to whom the deceased has directed the distribution of his or her assets.

DICTUM — A part of a *decision* of a court that is not the law of the case. For example, in the decision the court may refer to facts that are not involved in this case and gratuitously set fort the law in those situations. Such statements of law are referred to as dictum.

DIRECT EXAMINATION — The testimony given at a court hearing or deposition by a party or witness that is elicited by the party's attorney or the attorney who called the witness. During direct examination a witness cannot be asked *leading questions.*

DIRECTED VERDICT — After all the testimony has been heard by a jury and judge, the judge can find that the testimony is overwhelmingly in favor of one party. He may then direct a decision in favor of that party without allowing the jury to make an independent decision.

DISABILITY — An injury that is temporary or permanent. It is also used as a description of a natural condition that prevents people from having full control of their physical and emotional lives, such as a person being a *minor* or *mentally incompetent.*

DISBAR — When an attorney is stopped from the further practicing of law. Determined by a *proceeding* by a *tribunal,* established by statutory authority.

DISCHARGED IN BANKRUPTCY — At the conclusion of a *bankruptcy proceeding,* the judge can end the rights of creditors named in the bankruptcy to bring any further proceedings to collect their debts.

DISCLAIMER — The refusal to acknowledge the validity of a *claim.* Also the refusal of a person to accept property that has been given as a gift or by will.

DISCONTINUANCE — The terminating of a lawsuit by agreement between the parties or by the court's directive.

DISCOVERY — The legal process that takes place prior to a trial, where both parties are given the opportunity to examine all the evidence and to conduct *depositions* of all parties and witnesses.

DISCRIMINATION — The act of granting or denying a right to one person solely on the basis of race, sex, age, religion, national origin, and/or sexual orientation.

DISINHERITANCE — The act of a person who made a will or trust that provides no distribution of property to an heir. Generally, a person can disinherit any heir except a spouse.

DISMISS — The termination of a lawsuit by a court order. This can be done before or after trial.

DISPOSITION — The status of a particular case. Cases may be marked "ready for trial," "ready for conference," "settled," and "adjourned."

DISPOSSESS — The act of terminating the *tenancy* of a tenant of *real property* by lawful court means. This requires instituting a *landlord-tenant action* so that the tenant knows of the action and has an opportunity to present a defense.

DISSENT — In an appellate court, the opinion of a minority of judges who disagree with the decision of the majority of judges. The majority and minority decisions are rendered after the judges have an opportunity to review the facts and law of the case.

DISSOLUTION — The act of terminating a marriage, partnership, corporation, or business venture by *agreement* or by court order.

DISTRICT ATTORNEY — The representative of the state in all criminal cases who is charged with the prosecution of all persons charged with a crime.

DIVORCE — The termination of a marriage based on the laws of the state that are applicable under a court order. Divorces can be *contested* and *uncontested*.

DOCKET — A list of all cases that a court clerk maintains for the purpose of controlling the court calendar.

DOCTOR-PATIENT PRIVILEGE — A rule of law that says a doctor cannot disclose to anyone, including a court, information received from the patient without the prior approval of the patient.

DOCTRINE — A rule or theory of law.

DOING BUSINESS AS (DBA) — A phrase used to indicate that a named person or corporation is conducting business under an assumed name.

DOMICILE — The permanent residence of a person.

DONEE — The receiver of a gift.

DONOR — The giver of a gift.

DOUBLE INDEMNITY CLAUSE — A feature in a life insurance policy that provides that in the event the insured dies as a result of an accident, the insurance carrier will pay twice the face amount of the policy.

DOUBLE JEOPARDY — A doctrine that prevents a defendant from being charged more than once with the same crime. If a person charged with a crime is found not guilty, that person cannot be tried again for the same crime.

DOWER — The automatic right of a wife to reside for her lifetime in the marital residence after the death of the husband. This right is not applicable in all states.

DRAFT — A promise in writing to pay an amount of money when the document is presented for payment at a bank.

DRAM SHOP ACT — A statutory law that says that a person who dispenses alcoholic beverages to a person who is intoxicated will be responsible and liable for damages in the event the intoxicated person has an accident resulting from his intoxication.

DRAWEE — The party to whom a check is made payable.

DRAWER — The party who issues a check on their own checking account.

DUE PROCESS — The conducting of an impartial hearing to resolve a dispute between two or more parties.

E

EASEMENT — A right that an owner of land gives to another to use his or her property for a specific purpose.

EMANCIPATION — The date that a minor reaches the majority age (adulthood). Depending on state law, this can be at age 18, age 21, or at marriage.

EMBEZZLEMENT — The illegal taking of property of another by deceit. In most cases, the person who loses the property is unaware that a theft is taking place and may voluntarily turn the property over to the thief.

EMINENT DOMAIN — The right of a government to take *real property* for its own purposes. The government must pay adequate compensation, which is determined by a court if the parties cannot agree.

EMPLOYER — A party that hires one or more individuals (*employees*) to perform services for a fee under the direction of the hiring party.

EMPLOYEE — An individual hired by a party (*an employer*) to perform services for a fee as directed by the employer.

ENCUMBRANCE — A *lien* or *agreement* that is filed with the *registrar of deeds*, which notifies the public that the title to *real* or *personal property* is subject to claims of others. The lien may be a mortgage that has been filed with registrar of deeds. An agreement may be a right given to another to use the property (see *easement*) that is filed with the registrar of deeds.

ENDORSEMENT — The signature of the person to whom a check is payable placed on the back of the check for deposit. The endorser guarantees to the bank that if the check is not paid, he or she will reimburse the bank for any losses.

ENDOWMENT — A fund of money usually established for a charity that permits the charity to use the income from the principal for a specific purpose.

ENTITY — A form of business relationship, such as a *sole proprietorship, corporation, partnership*, or *limited partnership*.

ENTRAPMENT — A defense used in criminal cases where the government has established an illegal activity to ensnare persons who have a propensity to commit the illegal activity.

EQUITABLE DISTRIBUTION — The statute that grants a spouse at the termination of the marriage the right to acquire a share of the assets that were accumulated by the other spouse during the marriage. The precise share is determined by viewing the length of the marriage, the age and health of both spouses, and the income of both spouses.

EQUITY — The power of the court to direct against a party specific actions in the interest of justice.

ESCHEAT — The transfer of property to the state as a result of the abandonment of property or the inability to locate heirs. In some states bank accounts in which there are no deposits or withdrawals for a period of five years are automatically transferred to the state. The state will return these monies if an individual comes forward to collect them.

ESCROW — A sum of money held pending the *closing* of title to *real* or *personal property*. The purpose is to permit the purchaser to examine the *title* after signing a contract of sale and before the closing.

ESCROWEE — The person who holds escrow funds, usually an attorney or a *title* company.

ESTATE — The assets of a person who is deceased. This includes real property, personal property, life insurance, bank accounts, and monies due the deceased from others.

ESTATE TAX — A tax paid after a person dies. The tax is a percentage of the gross assets after deducting all debts and administrative expenses.

ESTOPPEL — A doctrine that prevents a party from making a claim once the party has committed an act that has caused another to change position. For example, if a party were to transfer real property at a time when he did not have full title. He or she can not claim at a later time when full title is acquired that the transfer was not valid.

ET AL — Latin for "and others." A term following a name in a lawsuit that indicates there are additional parties.

ET ANO — Latin for "and another." A term following a name in a lawsuit that indicates there is one additional party.

EVICTION — The act of removing a tenant from the occupancy of the *real property* pursuant to a court order. Generally, the tenant must be removed by a sheriff or marshal.

EVIDENCE — The testimony of parties and witnesses and the documents, photographs, and physical facts submitted at a hearing to determine the facts in a dispute.

EXAMINATION BEFORE TRIAL — The oral questioning under oath of a party or witness prior to trail. The questions and answers are recorded for future use in the trial.

EXCEPTION — During the course of a trial, a judge is called upon to issue rulings as to the admissibility of evidence. Whenever a party disagrees with a judge's ruling, the party can state on the record—before the court reporter—that they take "exception" to the judge's ruling. This preserves their right on appeal to have the appellate court review the ruling and possibly reverse the lower court.

EXCULPATORY CLAUSE — A paragraph in a will or trust stating that if an *executor* or *trustee* acts in good faith he will not be held personally responsible for errors in judgment.

EXECUTE A DOCUMENT — To sign a will, deed, or agreement pursuant to the applicable law. For example, a will must be signed in front of two witnesses; a deed must be signed before a notary who acknowledges the signature; an agreement must be signed at the end of all written text.

EXECUTIVE CLEMENCY — The power of the President or the governor of a state to reduce the period of time that one who has been convicted of a crime must spend in jail.

EXECUTOR/EXECUTRIX — A person appointed in a will who is granted the power to gather the assets of the estate, pay the outstanding bills, pay the cost of burial, and distribute the balance of the assets to the beneficiaries. An executor is a male and executrix is a female.

EXECUTOR'S COMMISSIONS — By statute an executor is entitled to be paid for his efforts. The payment is a percentage of the estate, generally 4 to 5 percent of the assets.

EXEMPLIFIED COPY — A copy of a document that is authenticated as a true copy.

EXHIBIT — A document, photograph, or other physical evidence offered as proof at a hearing. The court reporter labels and identifies each exhibit by number or letter.

EX PARTE — An application by a party to the court to issue an order without notice to anyone. The court will only issue an order without notice on very rare occasions.

EX PARTE DIVORCE — A divorce obtained by one spouse where the other spouse has failed to answer the summons or to appear at the trial.

EXPERIENCE RATING — A charging of an insurance premium, based on the prior claim history of the insured. The premiums are adjusted thereafter on the basis of the subsequent history of the insured.

EXPERT WITNESS — A person who testifies at a court *hearing* or *deposition* on behalf of one party about a subject not commonly known to the average person. The expert witness may be paid by the party who asks him or her to testify. The expert has some special training or education that qualifies him to testify.

EX POST FACTO — A law that takes effect on a specific date prior to the date that the legislature enacted the law. In criminal cases laws cannot be predated; the law must be in existence on the date the criminal act occurs.

EXPRESS AUTHORITY — The power specifically given, either in writing or orally, by one person to another. These powers are usually given by an *employer* to an *employee* or by one to an *independent contractor*.

EXTORTION —The obtaining of money from another by illegally using threats and/or violence.

EXTRADITION — The procedure to return a fugitive charged with a crime to the authorities where the crime occurred for the purpose of standing trial.

EYEWITNESS — A person who actually observed the happening of an event.

F

FACTOR — A person who lends money to a business and receives in return a *lien* on the outstanding *accounts receivable* of the business. The accounts receivable are then paid directly to the factor and thus the factor's loan is paid off.

FACTORING — The pledging by a business of *accounts receivable* for the purpose of securing the repayment of a loan.

FALSE ARREST — Depriving a person of the freedom to move about without legal grounds.

FALSE CLAIM — The setting forth of a claim by a party against another with the knowledge that the claim has no basis in fact.

FALSE IMPRISONMENT — Depriving a person of the freedom to move about by illegal incarceration.

FAMILY COURT — A court that has jurisdiction over family matters such as custody, alimony, maintenance, child support, adoption, juvenile delinquency, child abuse, and spousal abuse. The exact jurisdiction of the court is set by state law.

FAULT — The requirement that a spouse instituting an action for divorce, annulment, or separation prove that the other committed an act that is not permitted by statute and is grounds for the termination of the marriage.

FEATHERBEDDING — The requirement by a union that an employer employ more people then is necessary to perform a particular job function. This enables the union to put more people to work.

FEE SIMPLE — A form of ownership of *real property* where the ownership continues forever with the right to transfer ownership to another at anytime. Upon the death of the person the property passes to the heirs.

FELON — A person convicted of a crime that requires a penalty of more than one year in jail.

FELONY — A crime that requires a penalty of more than one year in jail.

FELONY MURDER — The death of a person during the commission of a *felony* crime. All person involved in a felony crime are equally guilty of felony murder if a death occurs during the commission of a crime.

FIDUCIARY — A person who is given authority, either by a court or by another person, to exercise control over assets of another. The person is required to safeguard the assets.

FILIATION — The determination that a man is the father of a child by a court.

FINANCIAL DISCLOSURE — An accounting of the income, assets, and liabilities of an individual or a business entity.

FINDING OF FACT — A judge or jury first hears all the facts in a case. They then review the undisputed and disputed facts and determine which facts they believe. The verdict or decision results from this process.

FINDING OF LAW — When a judge determines the applicable law in a particular case. If there is a dispute as to applicable law it is common for the judge to permit the parties to submit *memorandums of law* setting forth their interpretation of the applicable law.

FINE — A monetary penalty imposed by a judge after a plea of guilty or when a determination of guilt is made.

FIRE INSURANCE — An insurance policy that pays the insured in the event he/she has a fire loss.

FIRM — The name given to a group of attorneys who have joined together to practice law as either a partnership or a professional corporation.

FIRM OFFER — A promise to buy or sell property at a specific price, which is binding during a specific time period. If no time period is set forth, then, it is binding for a reasonable period of time.

FIRST MORTGAGE — A loan by which the borrower guarantees the repayment of the loan by granting a *lien* against *real property*. If the borrower fails to pay, the lender has the right to sell the real property.

FIXTURE — An item of personal property that is permanently affixed to *real property*, such as an oil or gas burner.

FLAG OF A COUNTY CLERK — A certification attached to a notarial signature by the county clerk authenticating the notary public's signature and right to notarize signatures.

FLOOD INSURANCE — An insurance policy that pays the insured if damage results from a flood.

FORBEARANCE — When a creditor waits for payment of a debt after a *default* rather then declaring a default.

FOR DEPOSIT ONLY — An *endorsement* placed on a check requiring that the check be deposited in the account of the person who wrote this on the check.

FORECLOSURE — An action in which a lender obtains from a borrower who has failed to repay the loan the property that was given as security at the time the loan was advanced.

FOREIGN CORPORATION — A *corporation* formed under the laws of a state other than the state in which the business is located. For example, many publicly traded corporations are incorporated in Delaware because it has no corporate income tax and the costs of establishing and maintaining the corporation are less than in other states.

FORESEEABILITY — A *doctrine* concerning accidents that pertains to acts that could reasonably be expected to cause injury to another. For example, it is forseeable that if one does not repair the brakes to a vehicle that the vehicle would have an accident.

FORFEITURE — If a person is charged and/or convicted of a specific crime, certain property or assets belonging to that person can be taken by the state. There must be a specific statute that permits this for a specific type of crime.

FORGERY — The act of intentionally signing the signature of another or otherwise altering a document for a criminal purpose.

FOR VALUE RECEIVED — Obtaining property from another by the payment of money or something of value to the person transferring ownership of the property.

FOSTER CHILD — A child placed with a legal guardian by a court or governmental agency. This is usually done to serve the best interests of the child. The child has no right of inheritance except if actually named in the will of the guardian.

FOSTER PARENT — A temporary legal guardian of a child who has been displaced from his or her natural parents by a court or governmental agency. Generally, the foster parent raises the child and receives money from the state to pay for the child's food, clothing, and maintenance.

FRANCHISE — The rights given by one business to another to use its name and business expertise in the operation of the same business at another location. The franchiser receives a percentage of the sales.

FRAUD — The act of intentionally deceiving another for the purpose of obtaining the other's property.

FRAUDULENT CONVEYANCE — A transfer of the ownership of *real* or *personal property* to another for the purpose of avoiding paying a debt. For example, a debtor who transfers his property to a relative so that a creditor cannot seize the property.

FREE AND CLEAR TITLE - When ownership of a property is transferred with all rights to it intact and all debts on it paid.

FREEDOM OF INFORMATION ACT — A federal statute that gives all citizens the right to examine all information compiled on them by the federal government. Classified documents are excluded for national security reasons.

FREEDOM OF THE PRESS — The right of the press to print any story without the prior approval of the government, or any individual.

FREEDOM OF RELIGION — The right to choose personal religious beliefs and to deny the government the power to establish a state religion.

FREEDOM OF SPEECH — The right of any person to say any statement without the prior approval of the government, or any individual.

FRESH PURSUIT — The right of the police from one jurisdiction to chase an alleged criminal fleeing apprehension into another jurisdiction.

FRONTAGE — The portion of *real property* that abuts the street or roadway.

FUGITIVE — An alleged criminal who has failed to surrender to authorities or, after surrendering, has failed to appear as required in court. A person who has been convicted of a crime and who escapes from custody is also a fugitive.

FULL AGE — The age when a minor become an adult In most jurisdictions it is age 18 or 21.

FULL FAITH AND CREDIT CLAUSE — The constitutional mandate that every state must enforce the judgment of another state.

FUTURE INTEREST — A right or interest in a property that takes effect on a specific future date or on the occasion of a specific future event.

G

GAG ORDER — An order issued by a judge that limits the comments that an attorney or party can make to the general public about a particular case.

GARAGEMAN'S LEIN — The right of a person who repairs a vehicle to hold the vehicle until he is paid. If the repairer is not paid, he or she can sell the vehicle at a public auction and retain the money due plus the cost of sale. Prior to the sale, notice must be given to the public of the sale; this notice usually appears in a local newspaper.

GARNISHMENT — This happens when a *creditor attaches* the salary of a *debtor* who has defaulted on a payment. The creditor can collect the unpaid balance, with interest, from the employer of the debtor, who will in turn reduce the debtor's salary by the amount paid. Generally, the debtor must first be given the right to repay the debt.

GARNISHEE — The *debtor* whose salary is *attached*.

GARNISHOR — The *creditor* who attaches the salary of the *debtor*.

GENERAL CONTRACTOR — A person who agrees to build an entire building or project, engages subcontractors to complete various portions and is responsible for the work.

GENERAL PARTNER — A person engaged with another in a *limited partnership* for business purposes. A general partner is responsible for all debts incurred by the partnership.

GIFT — The giving by one to another of property without receiving money or property in return.

GIFT CAUSA MORTIS — A gift given in contemplation of death. Federal and state tax laws presume that all gifts made within three years of death are made in contemplation of death and the amount of the gift is included in the estate of the giver. (This presumption may be challenged by proof to the contrary.)

GOING CONCERN — The purchase of a business that is sold as a functioning and operating enterprise.

GOING PRIVATE — A *corporation* whose shares are owned by members of the public that repurchases the shares for the purpose of eliminating all public ownership.

GOING PUBLIC — A business owned by a few individuals that sells shares of stock to the general public. A business goes public so that the original owners can bow out or to raise money for the expansion of the business.

GOOD FAITH — The performance of an act in an honest manner without any intent of cheating.

GOOD SAMARITAN - A person who comes to the aid of another person who is in danger, without expectation of any monetary reward.

GOODWILL — The good name and character of a business as it is perceived by the general public.

GRACE PERIOD — The period of time after a payment becomes due during which the debtor has the right to make payment without being in *default*.

GRAND JURY — A group of ordinary citizens who determine if the state has the right to charge a person with a crime. Generally, they listen to evidence presented by the prosecution and determine if it is sufficient to warrant a trial. The grand jury only *indicts*; it does not *convict*.

GRATUITOUS BAILEE — A party who holds the personal property of another without expecting to receive money or property in return.

GRIEVANCE COMMITTEE — A group of people selected by the government and charged with reviewing complaints against attorneys that may lead to their *disbarment*, *censure*, or suspension.

GROSS NEGLIGENCE — A degree of *negligence* that shows a wanton disregard for the life or property of another.

GROUP INSURANCE — An insurance policy issued to either a group of *employees* or an association of people that insures all participants for life, disability, or health insurance.

GUARANTY OF A DEBT — A written promise by one person to pay the debt of another in the event of a default in payment.

GUARDIAN AD LITEM OF THE PERSON — A person appointed by the court to supervise a minor.

GUARDIANSHIP AD LITEM OF PROPERTY — A person appointed by the court to supervise the assets of a minor.

GUN CONTROL LAWS — Statues that supervise the sale of weapons to the public. They state who is eligible to purchase weapons and the types of weapons that can be sold.

H

HABEAS CORPUS — A court order directing that a person who is a prisoner be brought before the court to determine if the imprisonment is lawful.

HABITABILITY — The requirement that the premises of a leased *real property* are free of safety and health dangers and therefore fit for occupancy.

HARMLESS ERROR — A mistake made by a judge in the determination of the introduction of evidence in a case that has no important effect on the outcome of the lawsuit. Harmless error is not grounds for a *reversal* by an appellate court.

HEALTH CARE PROXY — A statement in writing authorizing an agent to make health care decisions in the event a person becomes physically or mentally unable to make those decisions for themselves.

HEARING — Proceedings, such as a trial, where the opposing parties are given an opportunity to submit evidence and to cross-examine witnesses and parties to the lawsuit.

HEARSAY — An offer of proof in a case by a witness who is not an eyewitness and who obtained the information from another person who claims to be an *eyewitness*. Generally, hearsay evidence is not reliable since the eyewitness is not before the court and the actual witness's account cannot be cross-examined.

HEIR — A person who would receive assets of the deceased in the event there was no will. This is determined by state statues. Also the persons named in a will who are to receive the decedent's assets are known as heirs.

HIGHWAY — A road available for use by the public.

HOLDER IN DUE COURSE — A person who has received a note or check of another in exchange for something of value without the knowledge that the maker has a reason for not paying the obligation. For example, he or she does not know that the person who signed and gave the note received in exchange for the note defective merchandise.

HOLD HARMLESS — An agreement to reimburse another in the event a third party makes a claim against the other. For example, in the sale of real property the seller may have a judgment against him or her. In order to permit the sale to take place, the seller will sign an agreement wherein he/she holds the purchaser harmless from the judgment.

HOLDOVER — A tenant who occupies the premises after the lease has expired.

HOLOGRAPHIC WILL — A will in the handwriting of the deceased that is not witnessed as required by statute. In some states it is not legal to transfer property with these wills.

HOME OWNERS INSURANCE — An insurance policy that protects the owner of a home for many different perils, including fire, storm damage, and protection from lawsuits instituted for accidents against the homeowner.

HOMICIDE — A crime which is without justification resulting in the death of another.

HONORARIUM — A sum of money paid gratuitously, or a gift given to a person that is not compensation or salary for services performed.

HORNBOOK LAW — A reference to a particular statement of law that is not in dispute and is generally accepted as the law. Traditionally in the teaching of law, there have been books produced that set forth the basic law. These books do not set forth the law by decisions that illustrate the law but rather in a dogmatic style.

HOSTILE WITNESS — A witness at a hearing who might have an adverse interest in the case. Once a witness is determined to be hostile, the court will permit greater leniency in the questioning. Generally, a lawyer cannot ask argumentative or leading questions of his or her own witness. If a witness is deemed hostile, however, then these types of questions can be asked.

HOUSING COURT — A court established to determine disputes between landlords and tenants. It generally deals with collections of rents, termination of tenancies, building violations, and illegal occupancies.

HUNG JURY — A jury unable to render a verdict because of a dispute among the jurors as to the *findings of fact*.

HUSBAND-WIFE PRIVILEGE — The right of a spouse in a criminal proceeding to prevent the testimony of the other spouse at the trial.

I

IMPANEL — The act of qualifying a group of individuals to serve as jurors in a particular case.

INDEMNIFICATION — An agreement where one party agrees to cover the cost of another if they are sued by a third.

INDEPENDENT CONTRACTOR — A party who is requested to do work who is not an *employee.* An independent contractor is not an employee if the work can be done without the supervision of the party who engaged him/her.

ILLEGAL — An act that interferes with the life or property of another without justification or authorization.

ILLEGITIMATE — A person who has been born out of wedlock.

IMMIGRATION — Moving permanently from one country to another country.

IMMUNITY — A waiver that can be given by the government exempting a person from prosecution if that person agrees to testify about his or her part in a criminal activity. This is done for the purpose of getting one criminal to testify against another whose conviction is more important to society.

IMPEACHMENT — The act of removing an elected official from his or her position as a result of being found guilty of a criminal act.

IMPLEADER — Once an *action* is instituted against a defendant, the defendant has a right to bring into the lawsuit other persons who are responsible. For example, if two persons cause an accident and only one is sued. The person sued can bring the other into the action.

IMPLIED AUTHORITY — The authority given to an employee or independent agent to perform his or her usual work. For example, a person hired to act as a salesperson has authority to exchange merchandise for money.

IMPLIED CONSENT — An agreement that is implied by *statute.* For example, the operation of a vehicle on the roads of a state automatically grants to the state, by statute, jurisdiction over the driver and owner of the vehicle in the event of an accident.

IMPORT DUTY — A tax paid on the importation of goods into a country. The purpose of the tax is to increase the sales price of the imported goods so as to give an economic advantage to locally produced goods.

IMPOUND — The taking of property by a government agency.

IMPUTED NEGLIGENCE — Under certain conditions, the negligence of a person can be charged to another. By statute, the negligence of an authorized driver is charged to the owner of the vehicle or the negligence of an employee is charged to the employer. Once negligence is charged to another, that person or business becomes responsible for paying monetary damages to the injured party.

INCAPACITY — A person who lacks the ability to manage their assets. A contract made by an incapacitated person is not enforceable.

INCOME TAX — A form of taxation whereby the federal and state governments annually receive a percentage of earnings from a person or business.

INCOMPETENT — A person who because of a mental or physical disability lacks the ability to manage his or her assets.

INCONTESTABILITY CLAUSE — A clause in a life or health insurance policy stating that after a period of one or two years, any untruthful statement in the application cannot be used by the insurance company to deny benefits.

INCORPORATE — The act of establishing a proposed *corporation*. One or more persons are required to file a certificate of incorporation and pay the statutory fees. Each state will then authorize the corporation to do business.

INDENTURE — A bond or note that a borrower signs agreeing to the repayment of a loan.

INFANT'S COMPROMISE ORDER — A court order permitting a parent or guardian to settle a claim for a minor.

INDICTMENT — A finding by a grand jury that charges a person with the commission of a crime. After a person is indicted, he or she is brought to trial for the offense charged.

INDIGENT — A poor person who may be given special rights to proceed in a lawsuit without having to pay any court expenses.

INDISPENSABLE PARTY — A party without whom the court cannot determine the rights of the other parties in a lawsuit, and therefore must be part of it.

INFANT — A person under the age of majority, which can be either 18 or 21 years of age, depending on the state where the person lives.

INFORMED CONSENT — A requirement that a medical professional must advise a patient of all the risks and alternative treatments, prior to performing a procedure.

INFRINGEMENT — The illegal use of copyrighted material without permission from the *copyright* holder.

INHERENTLY DANGEROUS — A product which by its very nature is destructive, such as gasoline or explosives. The law requires special handling of such products.

INHERIT — To receive money or property from a deceased person's estate.

INHERITANCE — The property or money received from a deceased person's estate.

INJUNCTION — An order of the court directing that a particular activity is forbidden. The injunction may be temporary or permanent, depending on the circumstances.

INJURY — The wrong or loss caused to property or to a person.

INJUSTICE — The failure of a court to render a decision according to the principles of law and fairness.

IN PERPETUITY — The transfer of property to a party forever. For example, the sale of *real* or *personal property* grants the buyer the right to own it forever.

IN PERSONAM — The court has authority to enter an order affecting a party's life and/or property. For example, the court can issue an order directing a party to sign a deed.

IN POSSESSION — The actual occupation of *real property* by an owner or tenant.

INQUEST — A hearing in a civil lawsuit, where a party has defaulted to determine the amount of damages and enter a judgment. In deaths arising from unusual circumstances, hearings are held to determine if a person should be charged with criminally causing the death.

IN REM — The court has the authority to enter an order affecting the party's property. The court has no power to direct the party to perform an act as in the case of *in personam*. Thus the court can take the property but can not direct the person to do anything.

INSANITY — A mental condition in which a person is unable to manage him/herself and/or property.

INSIDER — A person who has confidential information regarding a business transaction.

INSOLVENT — A person whose income and assets are insufficient to pay current expenses and debts.

INSTALLMENT CONTRACT — An agreement that provides for the payment or delivery of property at scheduled times.

INSURABLE INTEREST — One can only insure the life or property in which one has an interest through some relationship, ownership, or debt arrangement.

INSURANCE COMPANY — A business entity that issues policies under state authority that agree to make payments to one who suffers death, disability, injury, property damage, etc. Also referred to as the insurer.

INSURED — The person to whom an insurance company issues an insurance policy.

INTANGIBLE ASSET — An asset of a business that is not physical, such as an interest in a copyright, trademark, or invention.

INTENT — The performance of an act with the specific state of mind that one is knowingly doing the act.

INTENTIONAL TORT — An act done by one to another by design and resulting in an injury or damages to the other. For example, the physical striking of another by design.

INTER ALIA — Latin for "among other things." It is used in agreements as part of a sentence. Inter alia, this book contains definitions of phrases.

INTEREST — A sum of money charged by a lender for the use of money borrowed.

INTERLOCUTORY — A temporary court order or decree issued before the final determination of the issues in a lawsuit that preserves the status quo.

INTERLOPER — One who interferes in a personal or business relationship with no right to do so.

INTERNATIONAL LAW — The law governing the interaction among foreign countries. These laws have evolved from statues inacted by countries, by agreements among countries and resolutions adopted by international organizations like the United Nations.

INTERPLEADER — A lawsuit instituted by someone holding property of others for the purpose of determining the respective rights of the parties who claim the property.

INTERROGATORIES — A series of written questions set forth by one party. The other party must then answer the questions, swearing to their truthfulness. Oral interrogatories are similar to *depositions*.

INTERSTATE COMMERCE — Business activities carried on between two or more states.

INTERVENING ACT — An act that causes a result that is not reasonably anticipated. For example, if a moving car collides with a parked car, it would not be reasonable to expect that the parked car contains dynamite, and thus the damage caused by an explosion is not reasonable to expect. The driver of the car that struck the parked car would not be responsible for the damage done by the dynamite.

INTER VIVOS TRUST — A trust established during the lifetime of the creator, which take effect immediately.

INTESTATE — A person who dies without a will.

INTOXICATION — A person whose blood-alcohol level is above what the state has decreed is legal. Intoxication is not a crime, but driving while intoxicated is a misdemeanor and an arrest can be made as soon as the intoxicated person gets behind the wheel and puts the key in the ignition, even if the engine is not turned on.

INVASION OF PRIVACY — The wrongful intrusion into the personal and private affairs of another.

INVENTION — The act of discovering a new or useful improvement of a machine, process, or composition of matter.

INVITEE — A person who has been authorized directly or indirectly to enter the *real property* of another.

INVOLUNTARY — An act committed by a person under duress. The act would normally not be done if the person could exercise free choice.

IOLA ACCOUNT — A bank account established for the deposit of attorney *escrow* funds. In many instances attorneys are required to hold client's funds to insure the performance of a contractual agreement. These funds are deposited in attorney escrow accounts. Many state laws provide for Iola accounts, which divert the interest to the states.

IPSO FACTO — Latin phrase for "by the fact itself."

IRREVOCABLE TRUST — A fund established during the life of a person that cannot be terminated by the person establishing the trust.

ISSUE — All descendants of a person who is deceased without regard as to whether they are a child, grandchild, great-grandchild, etc. In a will the text may limit it to mean only children.

J

JOINDER — The uniting in one lawsuit of two or more independent claims disputed between the same parties. The claims are thus determined all at one time.

JOINT ACCOUNT — A bank account in the name of two persons. Each individual has the right to withdraw all the money once the account is established even if the other contributed all the money.

JOINT AND SEVERAL LIABILITY — If two or more persons are responsible for the payment of a claim, in some instances each can be separately required to pay the whole claim where the other has no assets. The claim may arise from a loan agreement, a breach of a contract, or an accident.

JOINT CUSTODY — The court grants *custody* of a child to both the mother and father, who may be separated or divorced. Each parent has a say in the manner in which the child is raised, educated, and medically treated.

JOINT LIABILITY — The requirement that when two or more parties are responsible, that each be party to a lawsuit that seeks to hold only one of them responsible. The can not be sued separately.

JOINT TENANTS — The ownership of property by two or more parties. At any time any party can demand division of the property or the sale of the property with the proceeds divided amount the owners. See *partition actions*.

JOINT TORT FEASORS — Two or more parties who are responsible for a *negligent* act that caused injury to a person or damages to property.

JUDGE — A person appointed or elected under state or federal law to determine issues of fact and issues of law.

JUDGMENT — The court order granting rights to one party against another party which may include the right to collect a sum of money from the other party. Judgments are registered with the *county clerk* and they automatically become *liens* on *real property* until the judgment is paid.

JUDGMENT CREDITOR — The party who is due money from a judgment.

JUDGMENT DEBTOR — The party who owes money in a judgment.

JUDICIAL NOTICE — In rendering a decision a judge may accept facts that everyone commonly accepts. For example, it is not necessary for an expert witness to testify that the sun rises each day.

JUMPING BAIL — An accused criminal who has been released on *bail* pending a trial and who fails to appear in court without some justifiable reason. The bail if forfeited in the event of a failure to appear.

JURISDICTION — The power and authority of the court to render a decision against a party to a lawsuit. See *in rem* and *in personam*.

JUROR — A person selected at random to represent the community at a trial. Once selected for jury duty, the attorneys have an opportunity to ask them questions and challenge them. See *voir dire*.

JURY — A group of people selected at random to represent the community at a trial. Statutory law determines the number of jurors; in most states, it is either six or twelve persons. Statutory law also determines the number of *jurors* who must agree to make a determination. Generally, in criminal cases it is a unanimous verdict; in civil cases it is a majority verdict.

JURY INSTRUCTIONS — After a jury has heard all the evidence at a trial, the judge informs the jury as to the law. The jury is required to accept that law whether or not they agree its reasonableness.

JUST COMPENSATION — A reasonable amount of money awarded by a court so that the *claimant* is in the same financial conditions. This places the claimant in the same position he/she was in prior to the event that is the subject of the lawsuit.

JUSTICE — a person appointed or elected (as determined by state or federal law to determine the facts and the law in a particular lawsuit.

JUSTICE OF THE PEACE — A local judge who has limited *jurisdiction* over criminal and civil matters. Criminal jurisdiction may extend to *misdemeanors* and civil cases involving sums up to $15,000.

JUVENILE — A person who is a minor and thus under 18 years or 21 years, depending on state law.

JUVENILE DELINQUENT — A *minor* who has been found by a court to require supervision or rehabilitation because of prior criminal activity or disobedient conduct.

K

KANGAROO COURT — A court biased in favor of one side in a case without regard to the evidence or the law.

KEOGH PLAN — A means of savings permitted by federal law that permits a self-employed person to put income into retirement plan that is not subject to income taxes.

KETUBAH — A Jewish contract of marriage signed by the bride and groom and two witnesses at the time of marriage.

KEY MAN INSURANCE — A life insurance policy on an important *employee* in a business that generates large profits.

KIDNAPPING — The act of taking a person without his permission and demanding a *ransom* for his/her return.

KIN — A person who is related by blood to another.

KITING — The writing of a check without sufficient funds in a checking account to cover it.

L

LACHES — A *doctrine* of law that requires a claimant to act expediently in making a claim against another if the delay impinges on another's rights. For example, if a party knows that another will not have evidence if he delays bringing a lawsuit, then the delay in instituting the lawsuit may bar recovery on the grounds of laches.

LANDLORD — The owner of *real property* who rents it to a tenant for the payment of rent for a specific period of time.

LAPSE — To permit the termination of a right due to the failure to perform an act. For example, a lease may provide for notice to renew to be given thirty days before the expiration. The failure to give notice results in the renewal right lapsing.

LARCENY — The theft of property by one person from another. Grand larceny is usually over $500 while petty larceny is up to $500.00.

LAST CLEAR CHANCE — A *doctrine* that says even though an individual contributed to an accident, if the other party had an opportunity to avoid the accident and didn't, then the individual still may have a right to obtain money damages.

LAST WILL AND TESTAMENT — The final will of a *decedent* that disposes of all their assets according to the *bequests* made in the will. It also appoints an *executor* to gather the assets, pay all bills, and distribute the balance.

LATENT DEFECT — A defect that is not normally discoverable by a reasonable examination. For example, a structural defect to a building which is not visible is a latent defect.

LAW — Rules followed by a society, which include rules set forth in the Constitution, statues, customs, and precedent case law.

LAWSUIT — A claim of one person against another which has been instituted in a court of law.

LAWYER — A person who is authorized by the courts of a state to give legal advice and represent clients for a fee.

LEADING QUESTION — A question asked of a witness that tends to suggest an answer. Generally, lawyers cannot ask leading questions of his or her own party or witness, although they can be asked of the other party or witness.

LEASE — A written agreement between a *landlord* and a *tenant* that permits the tenant to occupy *real property* for a set period of time at a set *rent.*

LEGACY — A distribution of the assets of a *decedent* according to the terms of a will.

LEGAL AGE — The age when a *minor* becomes an adult. In most jurisdictions it is age 18 or 21.

LEGAL AID — A private nonprofit organization that renders legal services to poor or indigent people without charging a fee.

LEGAL PROCEEDINGS — A claim of one person against another that has been instituted in a court of law.

LEGAL SEPARATION — The act of a husband and wife separating and living apart according to an *agreement* or court order.

LEGAL TENDER — The money or currency of a nation that must be accepted for the payment of a debt or to purchase goods.

LEGATEE — The person who receives money or property according to the terms of a will.

LESSEE — The party who is the tenant according to a *lease* of *real property.* The lessee occupies the real property during the term set forth in the lease.

LESSOR — The party who as the owner of the premises leases *real property* to a lessee.

LETTER OF CREDIT — A letter, usually written by a bank, addressed to a seller of goods where the bank asks the seller to extend credit to a particular purchaser. The bank agrees to pay the seller in the event the purchaser fails to pay.

LETTERS TESTIMENTARY — A court order issued after the death of a person that recognizes the validity of that person's will as an *instrument* to transfer the *decedent's assets*. The order also appoints the *executor* of the *estate.*

LIABILITY — The responsibility of a party for acts that cause injury or damage to another party.

LIABILITY INSURANCE — An insurance policy that reimburses for accidental injuries to persons and/or property that are caused by the insured.

LIBEL — The making of a false statement in writing about another that causes harm or other damage when read or heard by a third party or parties.

LICENSE — A right given by one party to another to use another's property or name under certain conditions. A license can also be issued by a government agency for various reasons, including driving, car ownership, practicing medicine, and operating a business.

LICENSEE — The party to whom a *license* or right is granted.

LICENSER — The party who grants a *license* to another.

LIEN — A claim by a party on another's property that limits the sale of the property. A lien must be paid before the sale of the property can occur. In some cases the lien can be *bonded* by an insurance company so as to permit the seller to transfer the property at the present time and pay the lien holder at a later date, after all disputes are settled.

LIEN HOLDER — The party who has a claim against another who files a lien to protect his or her interests. Liens are usually filed with the *county clerk.*

LIFE ANNUITY — An agreement by an *insurance carrier* to pay a specific amount of money on a monthly basis for the life of an individual. The insurance company receives a lump sum of money and pays the money according to statistics that estimate the life expectancy of the individual.

LIFE ESTATE — The right of a person by agreement to reside in a particular premises so long as he or she may live.

LIFE BENEFICIARY — A person who receives periodic payments for a lifetime for a will, trust or insurance annuity agreement.

LIFE INSURANCE — An insurance policy that pays certain sums of money upon the death of a person.

LIMITATIONS, STATUTE OF — Sets for the number of years a claimant has to file a claim against another. Each state sets up its time period for each type of action; generally contract actions are six years and negligence actions are three years. In addition criminal statutes set forth the period of time in which prosecutions must be instituted.

LIMITED PARTNERSHIP —A form of business partnership with two classes of partners—general partners and limited partners. The general partners run the business and are personally liable for debts of the partnership. Limited partners usually are investors in the partnership and are not responsible for the debts of the partnership.

LIQUIDATION — A form of *bankruptcy* known as "Chapter Seven" in which the *assets* of the *debtor* are reduced to cash and to the extent possible the debts are partially or fully repaid and the debtor ends this particular business.

LIQUIDATED DAMAGES — Monetary compensation arising as a result of a breach of contract where the amount of money due can be precisely determined. For example, if a breach results in a loss of $1 per item, then the damages are $1 times the number of items.

LIS PENDENS — In certain types of actions a claimant can file a notice with the *county clerk* that automatically notifies the public that there is a claim against the property of the *debtor*. This restricts the debtor's rights to transfer property.

LITIGANTS — The parties to a lawsuit.

LITIGATION — The institution of a lawsuit in a court of law.

LIVING TRUST — A trust established by a person during his or her lifetime. The person establishing this trust may choose to retain full, partial, or no control over the trust.

LIVING WILL — A statement in writing authorizing an agent to make health care decisions in the event a person becomes physically or mentally unable to make decisions for themselves.

M

MAGISTRATE — Another term for judge.

MAIL FRAUD — The commission of a *fraud* by the use of the United States mails. For example, the requesting of money in a letter for a nonexistent charity.

MAINTENANCE — The monies paid to a spouse or former spouse for their support. The amount and the duration of the payments is determined by the assets of both spouses, the length of the marriage, the educational training of the spouses, and the age of the children.

MAJORITY AGE — The age when a minor becomes an adult. Each state sets their own age of majority, usually 18 or 21.

MAKER — The party who writes a check drawn on his or her checking account.

MALICE — Committing a wrongful act without just cause with the intent to cause harm, or where the court will imply the intent to cause harm.

MALICIOUS PROSECUTION — The act of instituting a lawsuit that is frivolous in nature and without merit.

MALPRACTICE — A term applied when attorneys, doctors, dentists, and accountants perform a professional act in an improper manner or with an unreasonable lack of skill.

MANSLAUGHTER — The causing of the death of another as a result of circumstances that indicate the death was not intentional.

MARITIME LAW — The set of laws that regulate the use of ships on navigable waters, including rivers, bays, seas, lakes, and oceans.

MARITAL DEDUCTION — The amount of the deduction allowed a spouse who has inherited *assets* from a deceased spouse. The deduction reduces the *estate tax.* Under federal law and in most states, all property transferred from one spouse to another by inheritance is exempt from estate taxes.

MARK FOR IDENTIFICATION — During a trail the court reporter marks physical proofs (*exhibits*) for identification. The witness is then asked to testify in reference to this proof and the court then rules as to its admissibility into evidence. See *mark in evidence.*

MARK IN EVIDENCE — Once a court rules that the proof is admissible, the court reporter labels the proof, "in evidence."

MARKETABLE TITLE — A *title* to *real property* that will permit a seller to transfer good and *clear title* to a purchaser without any liens or *claims.*

MARRIAGE — The uniting of a man and woman as husband and wife.

MARSHAL — An officer charged with collecting the *assets* of a *debtor* to satisfy a *judgment* of the court. An officer with the court's authority to evict a tenant from *real property.* Marshals and sheriffs have corresponding powers.

MARSHALING ASSETS — The act an *administrator* or *executor* gathering all the *assets* of a *decedent.* Also the gathering of assets by a *receiver* in *bankruptcy* proceedings.

MARTIAL LAW — A state of law wherein the ordinary freedoms of life and liberty are suspended because of some emergency situation.

MASTER — A party who employs others to perform services under his or her direction. An *employer* is considered to be a master.

MASTER-SERVANT RELATIONSHIP — Generally, an *employer* is fully liable for the acts of an *employee* that are within the scope of employment.

MATERIAL WITNESS — A person who can testify to an event who is usually the sole *eyewitness* and whose testimony is crucial in determining the true facts.

MATRIMONIAL ACTION — Actions between spouses for *separation, annulment,* or *divorce.*

MECHANIC'S LIEN — A lien may be placed against *real property* by a *contractor* who has performed work and who has not been paid. The lien is usually filed with the *county clerk.*

MEDIATION — A procedure by which the claims in a lawsuit are submitted to a third party for the purpose of settlement, so as to avoid a trial. The mediator is generally a former judge. The mediation can be binding or non-binding.

MEDICAL EXAMINER — A person employed by a local county government who is charged with the investigation of deaths that appear to be caused by other then natural causes.

MEDICAL MALPRACTICE — The performance of a medical procedure, treatment, or examination in an unprofessional and unskillful manner. A mere bad result is not sufficient to establish medical malpractice.

MEETING OF THE MINDS —The point at which a contract comes into being. Both parties agree on all the terms.

MEMORANDUM OF LAW — A statement of the law applicable to a case that is given to a judge by a party to a lawsuit for the purpose of assisting the judge in his review of the law.

MENTAL ANGUISH — The pain suffered as a result of a physical injury. This includes fear and anxiety.

MENTAL CRUELTY —The actions of one spouse that endanger the mental and physical health of the other spouse and that require the separation of the parties to prevent further injury.

MERCHANTABILITY — The requirement that goods sold are to be fit for the use they are intended. For example, an electric toaster will toast bread.

MERITORIOUS CAUSE OF ACTION —A claim that appears to be valid based on the proof of only the claimant.

MILEAGE — An allowance for traveling expenses that is paid at a set fee per mile traveled.

MINIMUM WAGE — An hourly fee set by federal and state laws that represents the least amount an employer can pay an employee.

MINOR — A person who is not yet either 18 or 21 years of age, as determined by each state.

MISDEMEANOR — A crime punishable by less than one year in jail.

MISCARRIAGE OF JUSTICE — A decision of a jury or judge which is contrary to the facts in the case or contrary to the applicable law.

MISTRIAL — An event that occurs during a trial that guarantees one of the parties cannot receive a fair trial. The trial is then scheduled for retrial before another jury or judge. A *hung jury* can also result in a mistrial.

MITIGATION OF DAMAGES — Every claimant must attempt to reduce his or her damages when either a breach of contract or injury to a person or property occurs. For example, when damage to property occurs, the party who is damaged must take steps to prevent further damage from weather and other conditions.

MONOPOLY — Occurs when one or two business entities controls the entire means of production of certain goods or services, leaving them free to set prices without regard to competitive forces. An example would be an electric company which is the sole producer in an area.

MONTH-TO-MONTH TENANT — A tenant who occupies *real property* owned by a landlord for one month at a time. To terminate this tenancy the landlord must give the tenant thirty days' notice in writing.

MOOT QUESTION — A question or claim before the court that is no longer in dispute since the parties have agreed to settle the claim or discontinue the lawsuit.

MORTALITY TABLES — A statistical analysis or actuarial table of the life expectancy of a person at a specific age.

MORTGAGE — A loan of money by a lender to a borrower that results in a *lien* on property, filed with the registrar of deeds, notifying anyone examining the *title* of the existence of the loan.

MORTGAGE INSURANCE — An insurance policy that pays the balance due on the mortgage at the time of death of the borrower.

MORTGAGEE — The lender of the money in a *mortgage* agreement.

MORTGAGE TAX — A tax due the state when a mortgage is recorded.

MORTGAGOR — The borrower of money in a *mortgage* agreement.

MOTION — An application, generally in writing, asking for a court order directing another party to submit to examination or to furnish copies of physical evidence. During trials oral applications are made in the form of motions to determine the admissibility of evidence.

MOVANT PARTY — The party who brings a motion before a judge.

MOVE THE COURT — The act of requesting a judge to rule on a particular question of law or fact. This is usually done in writing but can be done orally.

MUNICIPAL CORPORATION — A corporation established by statute that governs a city and has power to enact local laws and employ city workers.

MURDER — The taking of the life of another with malice and without justification or authorization of governmental authority.

MUTUAL INSURANCE COMPANY —An insurance company that does not issue stock and is owned by the policyholders.

MUTUAL MISTAKE — An error made by both parties to an *agreement*. For example, that an event will take place on a date certain.

MYSTERIOUS DISAPPEARANCE — Insurance coverage that pays if an item of value disappears under circumstances that are difficult to explain.

N

NATIONAL HEALTH INSURANCE — Health insurance coverage available to all legal residents of the United States regardless of their ability to pay for it.

NATURAL BOUNTY — The *heirs* who would normally inherit an estate. In order to make a will a person must know who is included in their natural bounty.

NATURALIZATION — The process by which a foreign-born person becomes a citizen of the United States and is then entitled to all the rights of a natural-born citizen except the right to become President of the United States.

NECESSARY PARTY — A party who must be included in a lawsuit. If a necessary party is omitted from a lawsuit this may result in a dismissal of the claim.

NECESSARIES — Items that are required for basic human life. For example, one spouse is responsible for food, clothing, education, and health care of the other. Generally, a minor is not responsible for contractual agreements except if he enters into a contract for necessaries that are to be supplied to him or her and he has the capacity to understand the agreement.

NEGLIGENCE — The accidental commission of an act that a reasonable person would not do.

NEGOTIABLE INSTRUMENT — An unconditional promise made in writing to pay money to the bearer on demand or on a specific date.

NEWLY DISCOVERED EVIDENCE — In certain cases a trial decision can be reversed if there is new *material evidence* that was not discoverable by prudent investigation.

NEXT TO KIN — The persons nearest to a *decedent* by blood, usually a child or grandchild.

NO FAULT DIVORCE — A divorce granted without the requirement of proving that one spouse committed an unlawful act.

NO FAULT INSURANCE — Automobile insurance coverage that pays medical expenses and loss of earnings regardless as to which vehicle was at fault in the accident. This type of insurance restricts the right of an injured party to sue in the event certain minimum medical bills, loss of earnings, or injuries are not incurred or sustained.

NOLO CONTENDERE — A latin phrase for "I am not contesting." A plea in a criminal case that sets forth that the person charged with the crime will not contest the charge. The penalty may be the same as a guilty plea but the accused does not have to publicly admit guilt.

NOMINAL DAMAGES — A token sum of money granted by a court.

NON-COMPETE CLAUSE — A section of an *agreement* that says that a person or corporation will not engage in a particular business activity in a specific geographic location for a specific period of time.

NONCONTESTABILITY CLAUSE — A statement in a will that limits a person's right to contest it. The will is contested, then the gift to that person will not be granted.

NONPAYMENT OF RENT — The failure of a tenant to pay rent in accordance to an *agreement*. This is one basis of *eviction* by a *landlord*.

NONPROFIT CORPORATION — A *corporation* established for charitable purposes.

NONSUIT — The termination of a lawsuit by a judge without ruling on the merits of the claim. For example, a lawsuit may be dismissed for the failure of the claimant to appear at the trial.

NOTARY PUBLIC — A person authorized by the state to administer an oath to a person signing a written document whereby the signer is swearing to the truth of the facts in the writing. An intentional falsehood would be *perjury*.

NOTE — A written document signed by a borrower that sets forth the terms of the repayment of a loan.

NOT GUILTY — A plea in a criminal case that advises a court that the accused did not commit the criminal act as charged.

NOTICE — See *actual notice* and *constructive notice.*

NOTICE OF CLAIM — A written notification to an insurance carrier that a party will make a claim according to the provisions of the insurance policy. Also, prior to institution a lawsuit against the federal, state, or city government a prerequisite is that a Notice of Claim be filed.

NOTICE OF PENDENCY — An official notice, usually filed with the *registrar of deeds*, that tells anyone searching *title* records that a claim is being made against a party. This is done in *foreclosure* of *mortgages* and of *mechanic's liens*.

NOVATION — The act of cancelling a debt by permitting the substitution of another party according to an agreement. For example, A owes B $500. C agrees to pay A providing that A cancels the debt against B.

NUISANCE — The unreasonable use of one's property so as to cause another harm.

NUNC PRO TUNC — A judge's request that an order be issued that takes effect at an earlier date. This is only done by consent of the involved parties or when it is shown that no one will be prejudiced by the granting of the order. For example, a statute may require a formal filing of a claim within a specific time period. The court on consent of the parties can extend the time period.

O

OATH — A promise to tell the truth. A person who testifies with an intentional falsehood would be guilty of *perjury*.

OBJECTION — An application to a judge by a party in a lawsuit that certain questions or testimony not be entered into evidence. Objections can also apply to *physical evidence*.

OBSTRUCTION OF JUSTICE — The act of interfering with the lawful activities of the police and government authorities.

OCCUPANT — A person who is in possession of *real property*. Tenants or owners in possession can be occupants.

OF COUNSEL — An attorney who is employed to render legal services on a particular case in conjunction with another attorney.

OFF CALENDAR — The removal of a case from the calendar by a judge. This may be done with the consent of all parties or the judge may do it if the parties are not ready to proceed to trial.

OFFENSE — A statutory violation of law that is less than a misdemeanor, such as a traffic violation.

OFFER FOR IDENTIFICATION — The request that a judge at a *hearing* permit *physical evidence* to be marked as an *exhibit*. Then questions can be asked of the witness to determine if the physical proof is admissible according to the laws governing the court.

OFFER IN EVIDENCE — The request that a judge at a *hearing* permit the introduction of physical proof into evidence. Once proof is accepted as evidence then the jury or judge can consider it in reaching a decision.

OFFER — The presentation of the terms of a contract for acceptance or rejection.

OFFICER OF THE COURT — A person designated by statute as a court officer; usually includes attorneys and bailiffs.

OFFSET — A claim by one party that the amount of the claim of the other party should be reduced.

ON DEMAND NOTE — A written *agreement* to repay a loan to the lender whenever the lender requests repayment.

ON THE RECORD — A statement or agreement made in open court that is recorded by the official court reporter.

OPEN COURT — A trial conducted in a courtroom open to the public. Generally, this is required in all trials except where the interests of justice dictate otherwise.

OPINION — The decision of a judge setting forth conclusions of law and/or fact.

ORAL CONTRACT — An *agreement* made between two or more parties that is not recorded in writing.

ORDER — A judge's written decision that directs a party to do an act.

ORDER OF PROTECTION — An order which may be granted by the court in *matrimonial actions* which prohibits one spouse from visiting the other spouse.

ORDER TO SHOW CAUSE — An application to a court for an order directing a party to appear before the court to answer a written *motion*. This is done to expedite proceedings when there is a valid reason to do so.

OVERREACHING — When a person in a position of trust uses that position to his/her advantage rather then acting in the best interests of the party whose interest he/she is supposed to protect.

OWNERSHIP — The exclusive right to possess, use, enjoy, dispose of, and transfer property.

P

PALIMONY — A *claim* for *maintenance* and a share of the assets of another where the parties have lived in a non-marital relationship.

PARALEGAL — A person who is not an *attorney* but who performs legal services under the guidance of an attorney.

PARDON — An order by the President or a governor that forgives a person who has committed a crime.

PARKING VIOLATION — A failure to adhere to any government regulation that regulates the flow of traffic by restricting the parking, stopping, and standing of vehicles.

PAROL EVIDENCE — The oral evidence given at a trial by a testifying party or witness.

PARTITION ACTION — An action where one party who owns a part of *real* or *personal property* seeks to have the property divided or sold.

PARTNER — A person who enters into an agreement with one or more people to engage in a business activity under a common name and share the profits according to an agreed upon formula.

PARTNERSHIP — A relationship between two or more people who agree to establish a business for a profit that will be distributed among them. Partners are each personally responsible for the *debts* of the partnership.

PARTNERSHIP LIABILITY — The responsibility of individual partners for the debts of the *partnership*.

PARTY — A person, partnership, corporation, or government entity that is a part of a lawsuit.

PARTY WALL — A common wall between two adjoining buildings.

PATENT — An exclusive right given to an inventor to own and sell his or her invention.

PATENT AGENT — A person who helps inventors obtain patents. The agent does not have to be an attorney but must pass a special patent agent's examination.

PATENT DEFECT — A fault that is plainly visible during an inspection of the property.

PATENT ATTORNEY — A lawyer who helps inventors obtain patents. This sort of attorney is required to pass a special patent bar examination.

PATENT PENDING — A notification to the public on merchandise that a patent has been applied for.

PATERNITY LAWSUIT — A lawsuit to determine who is the father of an infant; the outcome enforces support obligations.

PAWN — To deliver a *personal property* to a person who extends a loan in exchange for it. The property is held until the loan is repaid.

PAWNBROKER — A person engaged in the business of accepting *personal property* as security for a loan.

PAYEE — The person entitled to receive the funds represented by a *note* or *check*.

PAY TO THE ORDER OF — A restriction on a *check* that designates the specific person who will receive the funds.

PECULATION — The intentional misappropriation of property intrusted to one's care.

PEERS (TRIAL BY ONE'S PEERS) — Persons who reside in the community, are representatives of the community at large, and are of equal status to the party on trial.

PENAL LAW — The statues that define the various crimes and the penalties in criminal law.

PER CAPITA — The division of the assets of an estate by the total number of heirs, without considering the degree of separation from the *decedent*.

PEREMPTORY CHALLENGES — In the selection of a jury each party to the lawsuit has a specific number of jurors who can be excused without giving a reason.

PERFORMANCE BOND — a bond issued by an insurance company that guarantees a *contractor* will finish the work described in a *contract*.

PERJURY — The giving of a knowingly false statement that is either sworn to or affirmed to as the truth.

PERMANENT INJURY — An injury that will last the lifetime of the person.

PERPETRATOR — A person accused of committing a crime.

PER SE — In a lawsuit, when someone represents himself.

PERSON — A human being. In the law a person can also be a *partnership* or a *corporation*.

PERSONAL PROPERTY — Any property that can reasonably be expected to be moved from place to place. A house is thus *real property*, but a refrigerator is personal property.

PERSONAL PROPERTY TAX —An annual tax on the total *personal property* owned by an individual.

PERSONAL SERVICE — The delivery of a *summons*, *citation*, *petition*, or *order* to an individual by actually handing the document to the individual. State law usually provides for *substituted service* in the event an individual cannot be personally served.

PER STIRPES — The division of the *assets* of an *estate* by taking into consideration the degree of separation from the *decedent*.

PETITION — An application for a court order that states the reason an order should be granted.

PETITIONER — A person who signs and swears to the truth of the facts set forth in a petition.

PETITION IN BANKRUPTCY — An application to the *bankruptcy court* requesting that a party be declared bankrupt. Papers listing the *assets* and *liabilities* of the *debtor* are submitted, and all proceeding to collect any debts are automatically stopped until the bankruptcy court renders its final *order*.

PHYSICAL EVIDENCE — *Evidence* which is in the form of a document, business record, photograph, or goods.

PLAINTIFF — The party that institutes a lawsuit against another. The party sued is referred to as the *defendant*.

PLEA — The response of a person charged with a specific criminal act. The response is usually *"Guilty,"* *"Not guilty "* or *"Nolo contendere."*

PLEA BARGAINING — The reducing of a crime to a lesser crime so that the person charged will be encouraged to plead *guilty*. This assists the state by requiring fewer trials. The accused knows that if he commits another crime, he/she will not receive the same leniency.

PLEADINGS — The written complaint set forth by the party who institutes a lawsuit and the written answer or answers of the defending party or parties. The pleadings generally present the issues in a lawsuit.

PLEDGE — The giving by a borrower of some valuable personal property, such as jewelry, to another for a loan. The lender holds the property in his/her possession until the loan, with interest, is repaid. If the borrower fails to repay the loan, then the lender, after a specific period of time, can sell the property. This is similar to *pawn.*

POACHING — The unlawful entry onto *real property* for the purpose of capturing or killing wild life (fish and/or game).

POLLING THE JURY — After a jury renders a verdict either party can request the court to ask each juror in open court if the verdict concurs with their personal determination.

POSSESSION — The act of receiving property and exercising control over the property.

POWER OF ATTORNEY — A signed statement that permits a person to act for another with the full authority to financially bind the other person. A power of attorney expires on the death of the person giving the power. Not all powers of attorney are the same; thus each power must be read to determine the exact authority of the person.

PRECEDENT — A court decision that is followed by other courts in the application of law to similar factual situations.

PREFERENCE — When a court grants a speedy trial due to the advanced age of the *litigant*, a terminal illness, or because a person is receiving public assistance.

PREJUDICE — A bias demonstrated by one against another that may interfere with a juror or judge making a decision. All decisions must be based solely on the facts of the case.

PRELIMINARY HEARING — A hearing held prior to a criminal trial in which a judge determines that the state has sufficient evidence to prove a *prima facie case.*

PREMEDITATION — The commission of a crime with knowledge and intent to commit it. The penalties for premeditated crimes are usually more severe.

PREMISES — A parcel of *real property* including the land and the buildings.

PREPONDERANCE OF THE EVIDENCE — For a party to win in a lawsuit, its proof must be more convincing than the other party's proof.

PRESUMPTION — A doctrine of law that allows certain proved facts to be accepted as true unless evidence to the contrary is introduced. For example, a will is presumed to be valid; however, the presumption of its validity can be rebutted by offering evidence to the contrary.

PRIMA FACIE CASE — The elements of proof that are required to prove a basic case. Every *claimant* must provide evidence that will prove the basic elements of his or her case.

PRIME RATE — The lowest rate of interest charged by a bank to its most credit-worthy business customers.

PRIORITY OF CLAIMS — In a bankruptcy or foreclosure proceeding, each claim is assigned a lower or higher status. A claim that is a *lien* against property has a higher status and is thus paid before a general unsecured claim. General unsecured claims are debts which are not liens on specific property (such as a mortgage on real property.

PRIVILEGE — The right granted in special relationships, in which you are not required to testify against another, such as a husband-wife or attorney-client relationship.

PRIVILEGE AGAINST SELF-INCRIMINATION — The right guaranteed by the Constitution that allows an individual not to testify if the testimony will *incriminate* that person in a crime.

PRIVITY — The relationship between two parties in a contract.

PROBABLE CAUSE — Reasonable grounds that the person charged with a crime has committed the crime.

PROBATE — The offering of a will to the court for the purpose of accepting it as a valid will that can transfer the *decedent*'s *real* and *personal property*.

PROBATION — A period of time during which a person who has been found guilty of a crime is permitted to reside in the community under constant supervision.

PRO BONO — Performing legal services without payment of the fee. The latin phrase actually has three words "pro bono publico" which means for the "good of the public." Custom has shortened the phrase to "pro bono."

PROCEEDINGS — A hearing or trial before a court, *arbitrator*, or government agency.

PROCESS — A *summons*, *citation*, or *petition*, which when served on a defendant institutes a legal *proceeding*.

PROCESS SERVER — A person who is employed to serve *summons*, *citations*, and *petitions*.

PRODUCT LIABILITY — The responsibility of the manufacturer in the event its product causes injury to a member of the public.

PROFESSIONAL CORPORATION — A *corporation* in which all the shareholders are physicians, dentists, or attorneys. All claims against the corporation are subject to the limited *liability* protection afforded to corporate shareholders, except for *malpractice* claims and only personally against the person that committed the malpractice.

PROFESSIONAL SERVICES — Work performed by *attorneys* and/or *paralegals.*

PROMISSORY NOTE — A written loan *agreement* in which a borrower agrees to pay a sum of money to a lender at a specific rate of interest and at a specific time.

PROPERTY RIGHTS — The exclusive right to possess, use, enjoy and transfer an item of *real* and *personal property*.

PROPERTY SETTLEMENT — An agreement between two spouses to divide the property they own. This occurs as part of an *annulment*, *separation*, or *divorce*.

PROPERTY DAMAGE LIABILITY INSURANCE — A type of insurance that covers accidental damage to another's property caused by the insured.

PRO SE — A party to a lawsuit who represents himself, without an attorney.

PROSECUTION — The term applied to the District Attorney or U.S. Attorney in criminal court *proceedings*.

PROSECUTOR — An individual attorney who, on behalf of the state, is in charge of the trial of a criminal action.

PROSTITUTION — Performing a sexual act for money or property.

PROTECTIVE ORDER — A court order that restricts a person from having any social or physical contact with another. A spouse can obtain such an order if it can be proven that the mate will cause physical harm. The order is enforced by calling the police and exhibiting the order to the police.

PROVISIONAL REMEDY — An order issued at the start of or during a lawsuit that directs one not to transfer property during the course of a lawsuit. It must be demonstrated that the order is required so as to avoid irreparable harm to a party. For example, to prohibit a person from selling real property whose title is an issue in the lawsuit.

PROXY — A ballot that permits an absent shareholder to vote in a corporate election. The written ballot designates another to vote for the absent shareholder.

PUBLICATION — The act of advising the public of a fact. This can be done through the media or by certain filings with public officials, such as the *county clerk.*

PUBLIC ADJUSTOR — A person hired by the insured after a loss has occurred to assist in their claim against the insurance company. This is a very common procedure for fire losses.

PUBLIC AUTHORITY — A corporation established by *statute* that directs a newly formed governmental agency to engage in a business activity for the good of the general public. An example is the building and operation of a bridge by a public authority.

PUBLIC RECORD — The filing of documents with the *country clerk* which are maintained for the public's inspection.

PUBLIC UTILITY — A privately owned business enterprise that has no competition in its business operations, such as telephone, electric, or gas companies.

PUNITIVE DAMAGES — A sum of money awarded in a *civil suit* that seeks to punish the party, set an example for others, and discourage the act from being repeated. Depending on the case, there must be a specific *statute* that authorizes punitive damages.

PURCHASE MONEY MORTGAGE — A *mortgage* that the seller of *real property* receives instead of cash. The purchaser then makes payments to the seller of specific amounts of money with interest for the period of time stated in the mortgage. Part of the purchase price may be paid in cash and the balance may be the purchase money mortgage.

Q

QUANTUM MERUIT — A latin phrase for "whatever he deserves." If the parties to an agreement fail to specify a sum of money to be paid for the performance of a service, then the court will determine a sum that is reasonable based on time spent and the value received.

QUIET ENJOYMENT — The right of one who occupies *real property* as owner or tenant to be able to enjoy and use the premises.

QUIT CLAIM DEED — A *real property* deed in which one transfers to another all rights, title, and interest in the property without making any *representations* or *warranties.*

QUORUM — The number of people that must be present before a *corporation* or association can conduct business. The exact number is established in the by-laws of that specific corporation.

R

RAPE — The act of engaging in sexual intercourse without consent.

READY, WILLING, AND ABLE TO PURCHASE — Real estate brokers are entitled to a commission for their services when they find a purchaser who is ready to purchase, willing to purchase, and has the financial ability to purchase the premises on the seller's terms.

REAL ESTATE — Land and buildings and anything permanently affixed to the land and buildings.

REAL ESTATE BROKER — A person engage in selling *real property* for others and who receives a commission representing a percentage of the purchase price. Brokers are entitled to their commission when they find someone *ready, willing, and able to purchase.*

REAL PROPERTY — Property consisting of land and its buildings and anything permanently affixed to the land and buildings.

REASONABLE CARE — The degree of caution that an ordinary person would exercise in doing an act. A person is not free to do an act that will result in harm to another.

REBUTTABLE PRESUMPTION — A legal presumption that can be shown to be false by evidence and testimony at a trial.

RECEIVER — A person appointed by the court to take possession of property during a lawsuit in bankruptcy proceedings in order to protect the property and to collect the rents, if any. A receiver may be appointed even to operate an ongoing business.

RECEIVERSHIP — The term used when control of property is given over to a *receiver.*

RECIPROCAL WILLS — When two people make wills that provide for each other in a similar manner.

RECORD — The testimony and evidence at a trial is set down word for word by a court *reporter*, who then transcribes the account into a complete writing, is called the record. The record is used on appeal in the appellate court or by the trial judge after the trial to refresh his/her memory before rendering a decision.

RECOVERY — The amount of money or property obtained by a party as a result of a lawsuit.

REFEREE — A person appointed by the court to make determinations of fact after being given specific instructions who then reports the findings of fact to the court.

REFERENCE — The assigning of a hearing to a specific *referee*.

REFINANCING — When the owner of *real property* pays off an existing *mortgage* and in its place institutes another mortgage. This is usually done in order to obtain a lower interest rate or to obtain additional cash via a larger mortgage amount. For example, a person has an existing mortgage of $10,000. They obtain a $20,000 mortgage and use $10,000 of that amount to pay off the existing mortgage.

REGISTRAR OF DEEDS — A public official charged with recording *deeds* and *mortgages* so that the records can be searched by the public in order to determine who is the owner of *real property*.

REGULAR COURSE OF BUSINESS — Acts that are performed by *employees* that are routinely required by their *employer* in the operation of the employer's business.

REINSURANCE — A procedure where an insurance company that has issued a policy transfers all or part of the risk to one or more other *insurance carriers* in order to reduce its *liability* in the event of a loss.

RELEASE — A writing in which one party gives up all claims against another party. Once a release is delivered to another, all claims against that party terminate. A release is usually delivered as part of a settlement of an action.

RELIEF — The specific result that a claimant requests in a lawsuit.

REMAINDER — The part of an *asset* that still exists after a *beneficiary* has obtained income generated by the asset for a period of time, such as during that beneficiary's lifetime. This is a common provision in a trust or will. For example, the trust provides that a beneficiary receive the income from a particular sum of money during his or her lifetime. Upon death the remainder of the money goes to another.

REMAINDERMAN — The person who receives the *remainder* of an asset after a first beneficiary has received the income for a specific time period.

REMAND — The returning of a case to the trial calendar to await its being reached in the numerical order assigned for trial. From time to time a court may call the parties in a lawsuit for a conference for settlement purposes. If the case is not settled it is returned to its regular place in the listing of cases awaiting assignment for trial.

REMEDY — The specific result requested by a *claimant* in a lawsuit if the claimant successfully proves his/her case.

RENT — The amount of money paid by a tenant to a landlord for the right to occupy *real property*.

RENT CONTROL — Some states and local governments have laws that restrict a landlord from removing a tenant or raising the rent. This is done in situations where there is a severe shortage of available rental units.

REORGANIZATION — A form of *bankruptcy* known as "Chapter Eleven" where the *debtor* is given an opportunity to continue the business after the bankruptcy is completed. The court attempts to get a majority of creditors to accept a lesser amount of money or a longer period to pay off existing debts so that the business can survive.

REPLEVIN — An action brought in which one party who is entitled to possession of *personal property* requests the court to order another party who is unlawfully in possession of the same personal property to return it.

REPORTER — A person selected by the court to transcribe the testimony of all witnesses at a trial.

REPOSSESS — The taking back of property from another who is presently not entitled to possess it. For example, someone who lends money to another to purchase an automobile retains a *chattel mortgage* on the automobile and can repossess it if the loan is not repaid as required.

REPUDIATE — The act of terminating a contract between two or more parties as a result of a breach of contract by one of the parties.

RES — Lawsuits can be instituted to determine the rights of parties to the ownership of *real* or *personal property*. The subject party of the action is referred to as the res.

RESCISSION — A termination of a contract based on the fact that the contract was void at its inception.

RESIDENCE — The site where a person lives without any mental commitment that this will be the permanent living place of that person. For example, a vacation home.

RESIDUARY ESTATE — The remaining property after the specific gifts set forth in the will are distributed.

RES IPSA LOQUITOR — Latin phrase for "the thing speaks for itself." In instances when it is not possible to determine the exact cause of an accident, but the accident appears to be a result of negligence by one party, then the law establishes a *presumption* of negligence and the burden of proof is shifted from the claimant to the alleged negligent party. The alleged negligent party must then demonstrate that he/she was not at fault.

RES JUDICATA — Latin phrase for "the thing decided." Term applied once a court has decided the facts that were in dispute in a case and all appeals have expired. In any subsequent case between the same parties, the earlier decision is final and the earlier findings cannot be litigated again.

RESPA STATEMENT — A statement mandated by federal law that lending institutions must give *borrowers* when issuing a *mortgage* on *real property* as security for the loan. The statement sets forth the amount of the loan, the interest rate, and all charges.

RESPONDENT SUPERIOR — The doctrine that holds an *employer* responsible for the acts of an *employee*.

RESPONDENT — A term used in some types of proceedings to indicate the defendant or party against whom a claim is being made. In an appeal it is the party against whom the appeal is being litigated.

RESTITUTION — The act of making a party who has suffered loss or damage whole again. The responsible party pays damages that compensate the other for the loss.

RESTRAINING ORDER — An order that prohibits a party from distributing property or money to a debtor. For example, it would stop a bank from paying money on deposit to a depositor who is a debtor. It also may be used to stop a debtor from distributing property or money to another.

RESTRAINT OF TRADE — An agreement between two parties that interferes with free competition. This is usually done by fixing prices or restricting production.

RESTRICTIVE COVENANT — An *agreement* that prohibits the future use of *real property*. Recorded with the *registrar of deeds* as a public record, it usually prohibits the type of dwelling that can be built or the type of business that can be conducted on the property. A restrictive covenant in the sale of a business prevents the seller from engaging in the same business for a period of time in a particular area. A restrictive covenant in an employment agreement prevents an employee from competing with his employer after his employment terminates.

RETAINER — An *agreement* between a client and an *attorney* detailing the work that the attorney is to perform and the fee arrangement.

REVOCABLE TRUST — A *trust* that can be terminated by the party who established it.

REWARD — A sum of money paid for doing or not doing a particular act. Rewards are often used to obtain the identity of a person who has committed a criminal act or to obtain the location of a particular person who has committed a crime.

RICO STATUTE — A federal law that imposes civil and criminal *liability* for operating an organization that directs or commits two or more specified criminal acts within a ten-year period. The purpose of the law is to assist law enforcement agencies in their pursuit of groups engaged in organized crime.

RIDER — An addition to a contract that adds to or modifies the original contract.

RIGHT OF ELECTION — The right of a spouse to reject the provisions in a will and thus be entitled to receive a larger amount. State statutes usually provide a minimum amount due a spouse upon the death of a spouse.

RIGHT OF SURVIVORSHIP — A right of one party to the automatic ownership of *property* after the death of the co-owner.

RIGHT TO WORK STATE — Many states have laws requiring employees to join the union after being employed a certain period of time. Some states have right-to-work laws that give the employee the choice of joining or not joining the union.

RIPARIAN RIGHTS — The rights of landowners along a river to use the water of the river for personal and business purposes without denying the same rights to other, down-river landowners.

ROBBERY — The act of taking property from another through use of fear or force.

ROYALTY — A payment made for the right to use another's name, song, book, invention, property, etc.

RULE AGAINST PERPETUITY — Provides that a person may not set up a trust that lasts forever. This prevents a deceased person from controlling the use of *property* forever. The maximum period of time that a trust can extend is for the lives of a particular group of people, plus 21 years.

S

SALE — A transfer of the ownership of *real* or *personal property* from one party to another fro the payment in cash or other property.

SALES TAX — A tax charged at the time goods are sold by a retailer. The tax is usually a percentage of the purchase price of the goods.

SATISFACTION OF JUDGMENT — A writing that sets forth that a particular judgment has been paid and directs the *county clerk* to mark the judgment as satisfied in the records.

SCIENTER — The information a party has that is used for its benefit. Usually indicates that the information knowingly caused detriment to another.

SCINTILLA OF EVIDENCE — A small amount of proof that establishes a material *fact* in a lawsuit.

SCOFFLAW — A person who receives parking tickets and fails to pay them.

SCOPE OF EMPLOYMENT — The work that an *employee* does according to the directions of the *employer*.

SEAL — A wax impression, originally used on contracts and deeds as proof that the signature was authentic.

SEALED VERDICT — The determination of a jury that is put in writing and placed in a closed envelope. The jury can then disband and the judge can read the verdict to the public at another time.

SEARCH WARRANT — An order of the court that permits a police agency to search *real property* for evidence of criminal activity. The court signs the order after the police demonstrate that there is a probable cause that this proof will be found.

SECRETARY OF STATE — A state official who is generally charged with the licensing of *corporations* and regulating other business activities. (The U.S. Secretary of State is in charge of foreign affairs.)

SECURITY — The sum of money given by a tenant to a landlord as a deposit to ensure that the premises will be left in good condition upon vacating and that repairs or rent owed will be paid. The security is usually one month's rent.

SEDITION — Engaging in activities to overthrow the present government.

SEISIN — The possession of *real property*.

SEIZURE — Taking possession of *property* of another. A seizure may be legal or illegal.

SELF-DEALING — The improper use of property for one's own benefit by one who holds it in trust for another.

SELF-DEFENSE — The act of defending one's self from a physical assault. The law permits the use of only as much force as is necessary to repel an attack.

SELF-EMPLOYMENT TAX — A tax imposed on parties who are working for themselves.

SELF-HELP — The act of forcefully retaking one's own property if it is in possession of another who has no right to retain it. The courts look with displeasure on the use of self help and require persons to obtain court orders after hearings permitting the retaking by a person such as a sheriff.

SELF-INCRIMINATION — The act of being made to testify and by your own testimony being made to disclose facts that will find you guilty of committing a crime.

SENTENCE — The period of time that one convicted of a crime must spend in a prison or on parole.

SEPARATION AGREEMENT — An agreement between two spouses that provides they will live separately from each other. The agreement may provide for maintenance, *child support*, division of property, and *child custody*. In many states this agreement may permit a spouse after a specific period of time to obtain a *divorce* that is not grounded in the fault of either spouse.

SEQUESTRATION — The separation of a jury from family and the public to ensure that the jury makes its determination only on the facts in the case.

SERVANT — An *employee* who is paid by an *employer* to perform specific duties.

SERVICE — The institution of a legal action by the delivery of a summons to the defendant or a representative of the defendant.

SET-OFF — A claim that a defendant in a lawsuit sets forth against the party bringing the lawsuit.

SETTLEMENT — A voluntary agreement either not to institute or to discontinue a lawsuit because all the parties have come to an agreement.

SETTLER — The person who establishes a *trust* via an agreement that funds the trust, names the trustees, the terms of the trust, and the beneficiaries of the trust.

SEVER — The separation of one action from another action for the purpose of separate trials. Also, one defendant may be separated from another defendant for the purpose of separate trials.

SHAM — A transaction that is done for the purpose of attempting to satisfy a statutory requirement. For example, a debtor places assets in the name of another to avoid a creditor's rights to seize the assets.

SHAREHOLDER — A party who owns shares of stock in a *corporation*. Shares of stock indicate an ownership of a portion of a corporation.

SHAREHOLDER'S AGREEMENT — An agreement among the owners of shares in a corporation that generally sets forth the officers, directors, and the terms of sale of stock upon death or retirement of a holder of stock.

SHERIFF — A government official whose jobs include serving summons, guarding local prisoners, attaching and collecting property of debtors for creditors, and tenants for landlords pursuant to court orders.

SIMULTANEOUS DEATH CLAUSE — A paragraph in a will that establishes the order of death when persons (usually spouses) die almost simultaneously in circumstances where it cannot be determined who died first (usually an accident involving both spouses).

SLANDER — Making false defamatory statements about another.

SMALL CLAIMS COURT — A local court that generally has authority to settle claims up to $1,500. Individuals are able to institute cases without attorneys and obtain a speedy trial.

SOCIAL SECURITY — Federal laws that provide retirement and disability benefits for both employees and self-employed people. The benefits are funded by a mandatory tax on wages, which is paid by the *employer* and *employees*.

SOCIAL SERVICES — A financial assistance given to persons who are unable to work, cannot find work, or are permanently disabled.

SOLE PROPRIETORSHIP — A business entity owned by one person who is fully responsible personally for all the debts of the business.

SPECIAL DAMAGES — A sum of money that compensates a person for specifically identified losses, such as loss of earnings and medical expenses. General damages compensate a person for pain and suffering and permanent disability injuries.

SPECIFIC PERFORMANCE — A court order directing a party to do a specific act. For example, directing a party to transfer property to another. If the party fails to make the transfer, the court has the power to make the transfer and sign all the necessary documents.

SPENDTHRIFT TRUST — A trust established for a beneficiary that limits access to the funds in order to prevent the beneficiary from spending all of the assets at once.

SPLITTING CAUSES OF ACTION — Bringing an action for only one part of a total claim and then bringing separate action for the other part. The courts do not permit this. For example, if as a result of an accident one has a claim for property damage and another claim for personal injuries. Both actions generally must be brought together in the same lawsuit.

SPRINGING POWER OF ATTORNEY — The power to act in financial matters for another person based on the happening of an event, such as the disability of the person.

SQUATTER — A person who occupies *real property* without permission or authority of the owner of the property.

STANDING — A party who brings a civil lawsuit must be directly affected by the happening of an event. For example, a member of a minority group can not bring a lawsuit claiming discrimination unless that person was actually the target of the discrimination.

STATUTE — A law passed by both houses of the legislature and signed into law by the governor of the state or the President of the United States. The word statute and law are used interchangeably.

STATUTE OF FRAUDS — A state law saying that certain types of *contracts* must be in writing. These usually include contracts affecting the sale or leasing of *real property*, contracts that cannot be completed within one year, or contracts for over $1,000.

STATUTE OF LIMITATIONS — Sets forth the period of time within which a lawsuit may be instituted; for example, a breach of contract action generally must be instituted within six years and a negligence action within three years. Statutes of limitation also determine the period of time in which criminal prosecutions may be instituted.

STATUTORY LAW —The laws of a state or country that are passed by the legislature and signed into law by the governor.

STATUTORY RAPE — Sexual intercourse with a female under the age of 16, 17, or 18 years, depending on the particular state where the action occurs.

STAY — A court order that prohibits a party, a government official (such as a sheriff), or a third party from performing an unotherwise legal act. The stay usually lasts until the court conducts a full hearing on the issues and makes a decision permitting or prohibiting the legal act.

STIPULATION — An agreement made between two parties to a lawsuit that affects the lawsuit in some way.

STOCK — A share of the ownership in a corporation. The corporation gives the owner of the share a written acknowledgment of his or her interest in the form of a stock certificate which is signed by officers of the corporation.

STRICT CONSTRUCTION — The interpretation of ambiguities in a written agreement against the person who drew up the contract. Also, criminal statutes must be strictly interpreted to determine if a crime has been committed.

STRICT LIABILITY — Some parties are held to a higher standard of responsibility and thus the occurrence of an event results in their responsibility for all damages. For example, a business that uses explosives for demolition is strictly responsible for all damages without a showing of negligence or fault.

STRIKE — Employees refusing to work until they receive higher wages or better work conditions.

SUBCONTRACTOR — A party employed by a *general contractor* to do a portion of the general contractor's work under the supervision of the general contractor.

SUBLEASE — An agreement between a *tenant* and another where the *tenant* rents part or all of the *real property* to the other. The consent of the *landlord* is usually required, based on the *lease* between the landlord and the tenant.

SUBORDINATION — The permitting of one creditor to have a claim against a debtor that comes first in the order of payment. Thus the holder of a first mortgage has a superior claim to the holder of the second mortgage.

SUBPOENA — A directive that requires a party and/or records to be presented in court on a particular date and time. The failure to abide by the subpoena may be considered contempt of court and a judge may direct a sheriff to physically bring the party to court and/or punish the party who has disobeyed the subpoena.

SUBROGATION — The permitting of one party (the *subrogor*) to allow another (the *subrogee*) to bring a claim and lawsuit on his/her behalf. Normally, insurance contracts provide that when an insurance carrier makes a payment to its insured, that the insurance carrier is subrogated to the rights of the insured.

SUBROGEE — The party who is permitted to bring a claim and lawsuit on behalf of another.

SUBROGOR — The party who grants the right to another to bring a claim and lawsuit on his/her behalf.

SUBSCRIBER — A party who signs a written agreement and is then bound by its terms.

SUBSCRIBING WITNESS — A person who witnesses a signature on an agreement or document. This person is not bound by the agreement or document.

SUBSTANTIAL PERFORMANCE — Occurs when a party to a contract fulfills all the major requirements but through an oversight may fail to perform a minor technical requirement.

SUBSTITUTE EXECUTOR OR TRUSTEE — A party who became an *executor* or *trustee* as a result of the first named executor or trustee failing to serve, being unable to serve, or being deceased.

SUBSTITUTE SERVICE — The delivery of a summons, citation, or petition where it is not physically handed over to the person. State laws usually allow service upon a person by leaving a copy with someone of suitable age and mailing a copy to the person.

SUCCESSOR — A party who takes the place of another and assumes all rights and responsibilities.

SUMMARY JUDGMENT — A *judgment* obtained prior to a trial based on the fact that there are no issues in dispute. For example, if the claim arises from a written *note*, the claimant can ask the court on notice to the debtor that since there are no facts in dispute and the claimant is entitled to summary judgment without a trial.

SUMMARY PROCEEDINGS — The ability of a landlord to remove a tenant who has not paid rent or who has stayed over and beyond the lease or rental agreement.

SUMMATION — In a civil trail the attorney for each party has the opportunity after all the evidence is heard and before the judge charges the jury with the law to speak to the jury and highlight the evidence to show why their client should prevail. In criminal cases, the prosecuting and defense attorneys have the same rights.

SUMMONS — A document served upon a party for the purpose of notifying the party that a lawsuit has been instituted. It names the parties, their addresses, the applicable court, the attorney for the claimant, and the time for the party being sued to respond to the summons.

SUNSHINE LAWS — State laws that permit a party to see investigative reports of state agencies.

SURETY — A party who agrees to pay a named third party in the event another fails to complete the terms of an agreement.

SURETY BOND — An insurance policy in which the insurance company agrees to pay a named third party in the event the insured fails to perform an act, such as the completion of the construction of a building.

SURROGATE MOTHER — A woman who agrees to have a fertilized egg implanted in her body for the purpose of carrying the embryo to full term, at which time the baby is given to another.

SURROGATE'S COURT — A court that governs the distribution of estates of decedents who have or do not have wills.

SUSTAIN — During a trial or hearing a judge is called upon to rule on the admissibility of testimony and evidence. These rulings generally occur when one party *objects* to these admissions. The judge then listens to both sides and issues a ruling that sustains or overrules the objection. By sustaining the objection, the judge rules that the offered testimony or evidence cannot be heard by the court.

SURVEY — A plot plan of a parcel of *real property* that sets forth the exact dimensions of the land and the exact location of all structures on the land.

SUSPENSION — Temporarily stopping a party from performing a legal act. From time to time professionals may be suspended from practice for a set period of time.

T

TAX GRIEVANCE — Filing a formal claim that the assessed value set by the local tax department for a parcel of *real property* is higher than the assessed value of other similar parcels in the general area.

TAX LIEN — A claim against *real property* resulting from the nonpayment of either federal or state income taxes or local real estate taxes.

TAX RATE — The percentage that either federal or state governments collect for income taxes due. Also, the percentage of the assessed value of *real property* that the local government collects.

TAX SALE — The sale of a parcel of *real property* by a local government due to the failure of the owner to pay real estate taxes.

TAX WAIVER — A document issued by the Internal Revenue Service or a state taxing authority that permits the transfer of property after the death of the owner. The issuance of the tax waiver assures the payment of inheritance taxes.

TAKE-HOME PAY — The money that an *employee* receives for wages after deducting the federal, state, and social security taxes, unemployment insurance, disability insurance, health insurance, and pension benefits.

TELLER'S CHECK — A check issued by a bank that is similar to a money order or bank check.

TENANCY BY THE ENTIRETY — A type of ownership of *real property* by two people who are married at the time they take title. Upon the death of either spouse, the other receives the decedent's interest. Thus, when the survivor sells the property he/she only needs to present an official death certificate.

TENANCY IN COMMON — A type of ownership of *real property* by two or more people where anyone can sell their interest to a third party. In addition, they can force a sale or division of the property by bringing an action for *partition.*

TENANCY AT WILL — A type of occupancy of *real property* that can be terminated at any time by either party.

TENANCY FOR A PERIOD OF TIME — A type of occupancy of *real property* for a specific length of time.

TENANT — A person who enters into a rental agreement with a *landlord* that permits the person to occupy *real property* owned by the landlord for a fee paid to the landlord.

TENDER — The offering of money by one party to another.

TERM INSURANCE — A form of life insurance that covers an individual for a specific period of time. Generally, the premium increases every five years. This policy has no cash surrender value.

TESTAMENT — A document that if properly executed before witnesses, can pass *real property* and *personal property* to specific *beneficiaries* after the death of the person creating the document. This can also be called a will.

TESTAMENTARY TRUST — A *trust* established according to the terms of a *will* that takes effect on the death of the person drawing the will (the *testator*).

TESTATOR/TESTATRIX — The person who makes a *will* for the purposes of transferring property after death. Testator is the male form and testatrix is the female form.

TESTIMONY — Oral evidence given by a party or witness at a trial.

THEFT INSURANCE — An insurance policy that covers a person for theft of personal property.

THIRD PARTY ACTION — In some lawsuits a party who is sued may have claim against another arising out of the same transaction or incident. The other party is then brought into the action, which is known as a third party action.

THIRD PARTY BENEFICIARY — A person who is not a party to a *contract* but who benefits by the contract in some way. In certain circumstances the third party beneficiary can bring an action against one of the parties. For example, a child, due to an agreement between her mother and father, may have a right to enforce payments due for *child support*.

THIRD PARTY DEFENDANT — The third party against whom a defendant in an action brings a *third party action*.

THIRD PARTY PLAINTIFF — The defendant who institutes a *third party action* against a *third party defendant* is know as the third party plaintiff.

TICKET — A license that specifically permits a party to partake in a theater, sporting event, railroad ride, amusement ride, etc.

TITLE — The proof of ownership of *property*.

TITLE FEE INSURANCE — An insurance policy that gives coverage to a new owner of *real property* in the event the title searcher made an error in the search of the records.

TITLE MORTGAGE INSURANCE — An insurance policy that gives coverage to the holder of the *mortgage* on *real property* in the event the title searcher made an error in their search of the records.

TITLE REPORT — A search of the records that determines who is the owner of the real property and what *liens* exist against the real property.

TOLLING THE STATUTE OF LIMITATIONS — A procedure by which a *statute of limitations* can be extended. To toll the statute of limitations, generally, a *summons* and *complaint* must be delivered to either a court clerk or a *sheriff* within the original period of the statute of limitation. The *defendant* then can be served within 60 days after the original statute of limitations has expired.

TOMBSTONE ADVERTISEMENT — An advertisement of the offering to the public of shares of *stock* in a *corporation*. It is called a tombstone because the advertisements only permit very basic information—the name of the corporation, the price per share, the number of shares offered and the party selling the stock on behalf of the corporation.

TORT — A legal wrong that is committed against a party, person, or property that is not grounded in contract law. The legal wrong can be intentional or unintentional (an accident) and it causes injury to a person or damage to property.

TORT-FEASOR — A party that commits a wrong that is designated as a *tort*.

TRADEMARK — A symbol, name, or word used by a wholesaler or retailer to distinguish its products from those of others.

TRADE SECRET — A formula, pattern, or information used in a business and that gives the business an advantage and is unknown to a competitor.

TRANSACTING BUSINESS — In lawsuits and in the application of tax law, the determination that businesses are engaged in their usual trade in a particular state or locality.

TRANSFER — To convey property frights from one party to another.

TRANSFER TAX — A tax paid whenever title to *real property* is changed as a result of sale. The tax is a percentage of the selling price and is determined by state law.

TRAVERSE — A hearing before a court to determine if a summons was properly served.

TREASON — The act of attempting to overthrow the government, or giving assistance to any enemy of the government.

TRESPASS — The act of physically entering the *real property* of another without authority.

TRIABLE ISSUES OF FACT — A judge's decision that there are factual disputes between parties that must be determined at trial. In a trial the judge or jury can view the witnesses and their responses to determine credibility.

TRIAL — A hearing before a judge or *arbitrator* to determine issues of fact and law and where witnesses are called to testify.

TRIAL MEMORANDUM — A review of the facts or law in a case that is prepared by a party and given to the judge for the purpose of setting forth the party's factual and legal claims.

TRUST — A written *agreement* where a person places money or property under the control of another (known as a trustee). The trust contains specific guidelines for its use and may be *irrevocable* or *revocable*. The trust can take effect when the person is alive or after death.

TRUSTEE — A person who has been selected by another or a court to control the property or money of another for specific purposes.

TURNKEY CONTRACT — An agreement with a builder to build or restore a building and make it ready for occupancy.

U

U.C.C.-1 — A document filed under the Uniform Commercial Code to establish a claim against personal property. Generally, a U.C.C.-1 is filed with the *country clerk* and the Secretary of State of the individual state. After filing, the U.C.C.-1 becomes a public record and potential lenders and purchasers can determine whether there are any outstanding claims against the property.

ULTRA VIRES ACT — A business transaction by a corporation beyond the scope of the powers granted to the corporation. For example, a corporation may not have the right to purchase and sell real property.

UNCONSTITUTIONAL — A finding of a court that a particular exercise of power by a federal or state legislature or agency is not permissible according to the U.S. Constitution or a state constitution.

UNDERINSURED MOTORIST COVERAGE — An insurance policy that insures the owner and occupants of a vehicle whenever an accident is caused by another vehicle and the other vehicle has very limited bodily injury coverage (the other vehicle is thus underinsured). If the insured purchases underinsured coverage in an amount in excess of the limited coverage of the other vehicle, then the carrier will pay (if the injuries warrant it) a sum of money up to the amount of the full underinsured motorist coverage.

UNDERTAKING — An agreement by one party to a contract to perform a specific act according to terms of the contract.

UNDISCLOSED PRINCIPAL — A party who directs an agent to act on their behalf and further directs the agent not to inform others of his/her role as agent. It then appears that the agent is the principal.

UNDISPUTED FACT — A fact that the parties to a lawsuit do not contest.

UNDUE INFLUENCE — A claim that can be made by someone who is adversely affected by the contents of a will. It must be proved that another so controlled the maker of the will that he or she was unable to exercise independent judgment in the selection of beneficiaries and the distribution of assets.

UNIFORM COMMERCIAL CODE — A statute adopted by most of the states that sets forth the laws governing bulk *transfers*, *bills of lading*, sale of *personal property*, and liens on personal property.

UNINSURED MOTORIST COVERAGE — An insurance policy that reimburses the owner and occupants of a vehicle for bodily injury in the event that the vehicle that caused the accident was uninsured.

UNION SHOP — A place of employment where all employees are required to be members of a particular union.

UNJUST ENRICHMENT — The receiving of a benefit from another where that person receives no compensation. The law will require, generally, that the other be compensated. For example, if a house-painter is requested to paint a house without an agreement to be paid a specific amount he is entitled to be paid on a *quantum meruit* basis.

UNLIQUIDATED AMOUNT — Damages that are not specific as to amount; for example, damages for pain and suffering.

UNMARKETABLE TITLE — A finding that the title is not free and clear because of claims by other parties.

U.S. ATTORNEY — A federal official who is charged with representing the United States as prosecutor in federal criminal cases. These attorneys also represent the United States in civil claims against others and defend civil claims instituted against the United States.

USURY — The charging of interest in excess of state law. The entire debt becomes uncollectable if it is established that a debtor has been charged interest in excess of the permissible rate.

V

VACATE — To render an act of a court void. For example, after a judgment is entered, a court, for good reasons, may set the judgment aside.

VALUE ADDED TAX — A tax added to the price of goods at the factory. In many European countries it is common practice to have this tax in lieu of income taxes.

VARIANCE — An application to a local governing body to request the change of an existing zoning law as it applies to a specific piece of *real property*.

VENDEE — the purchaser of *personal property*.

VENDOR — The seller of *personal property*.

VENUE — The place where a lawsuit is instituted. Generally, a suit can only be instituted where one of the parties resides or does business or the place where the act occurred.

VERBATIM — A word-for-word transcription of a hearing or trial by a court *reporter*.

VERDICT — A decision by a jury or judge that determines issues of fact and law as applicable to all the parties to a lawsuit.

VERIFICATION — A sworn statement attached to a written document that claims the document is true.

VICARIOUS LIABILITY — The indirect responsibility of a party. For example, an employer has responsibility for the acts of employees done in the regular course of business.

VISITATION RIGHTS — The right of a parent or grandparent to visit with a child or grandchild. Visitation rights can be established by agreement, court order, or statute.

VOID — An agreement that by law is unenforceable. For example, an agreement to perform an illegal act such as agreeing to purchase an illegal substance.

VOIDABLE CONTRACT — A contract that can be terminated by only one of the parties. For example, an agreement between an adult and a minor is voidable only by a minor.

VOIR DIRE — The attorneys for the parties to a civil lawsuit or the prosecution or defense counsel in a criminal case are generally permitted to ask prospective jurors questions prior to the trial to determine if they might be biased toward a party in the proceedings.

W

WAIVER — The voluntary relinquishing of a right by a party.

WAIVER OF PREMIUM — A provision in a policy of either life, disability, or health insurance that keeps the policy in effect even though premiums are not being paid if the policyholder is able to prove an actual physical or mental disability.

WANTON ACT — An act done in reckless disregard of the consequences.

WARD OF THE COURT — A person under the age of either 18 or 21 is considered an infant or *minor* and is under the protection of the court. Thus the court must take special steps to protect the interests of the infant or minor whenever the court has jurisdiction over their rights.

WARRANTY — A statement in an agreement that a particular fact is true.

WARRANTY DEED — A deed transferring *real property* in which the seller guarantees to the purchaser that he or she has good *title* to the premises.

WELFARE — A sum of money paid by the government to enable impoverished people to feed, clothe, and house themselves.

WHOLE LIFE INSURANCE — An insurance policy that has a fixed annual premium. The policy generally has a cash surrender value that increases over the years, which the insured can borrow against.

WILL — A written document that if properly executed before witnesses can pass *real* and *personal property* to specific *beneficiaries* after the death of the person making it. A will can also be called a *testament*.

WITHHOLDING TAX — An income tax paid by an employee that is deducted from his or her weekly salary by the *employer*. The employer is required to turn over the money to the federal or state government.

WITH PREJUDICE — The termination of a lawsuit prior to the final determination of a court. A *discontinuance* with prejudice prevents the institution of another suit for the same claim.

WITNESS — a person who testifies at a judicial hearing.

WORKING CAPITAL — The cash that a business has on hand to continue its operations.

WORKERS COMPENSATION — State law provides that if an employee is injured in the workplace the employee has the right to receive earnings lost, medical payments, and permanent awards for personal injuries. The employer is required to have workers compensation insurance. The rate is effected by previous claims and the dangers involved in the particular job. The employee has the right to collect even if there was contributory negligence. They cannot collect if they intentionally injured themselves.

WRIT — An order issued by a court directing a specific act.

WRONGFUL ACT — The act of causing injury to another's life or property.

WRONGFUL DEATH ACTION — a lawsuit instituted on behalf of the beneficiaries of a decedent for the loss they suffered as a result of a death caused by the negligence or intentional act of another.

Y

YOUTHFUL OFFENDER TREATMENT — The sealing of criminal records committed by someone under sixteen after a finding of guilt. Thus the general public does not know that the minor was ever convicted of a crime. The age and law varies from state to state.

Z

ZONING — Local laws that govern the construction of buildings on *real property*. Zoning designates size, height, placement, and use of buildings.

NOTE ON THE AUTHOR

Stanford Altschul has been engaged in the general practice of law in the State of New York for thirty-four years. He graduated from New York University School of Law in 1959 and is presently engaged in the private practice of law in Mineola, New York. He is admitted to practice in the State of New York, the Federal District Courts in the Southern and Eastern districts of New York, and the United States Supreme Court. He is also an arbitrator for the American Arbitration Association, the District Courts of Nassau and Suffolk Counties, and is an Administrative Law Judge for the City of New York.